TERRIBLE LIFE-ALTERI
THAT HAVE FADED INT
HISTOR

Imagine a deadly terrorist bomb attack on American school kids. Or a sinking ocean liner that claims six times the number of lives lost in the Titanic disaster. Or an attack of deadly snakes on a town leaving fifty dead.

THESE THINGS HAVE ALREADY HAPPENED, BUT PEOPLE NO LONGER REMEMBER.

This is the premise behind *Forgotten Tragedies.* This eye-opening new book explores a number of tragic events, worldwide but mostly in the U.S. that have largely been wiped from public memory. These are tragedies with great human consequence, both at the hands of man and mother nature. These events include calamities which have faded into the fabric of time, but should be remembered for their level of heartbreaking catastrophe.

"One witness said the flood was like a 'huge hill rolling over and over.' A train engineer saved many lives when he saw the flood coming, by throwing his engine in reverse, whistle blaring, to warn the people, until the flood reached the engine and tossed it aside like a toy. The engineer survived, but at least 50 people on the train died."

"Long before cable news, these stories of diabolical minds and tremendous tragedy captured our hearts and united

America in hope and prayer. Updates crackles over the radio and blared from front pages. Bob's book captures these fascinating, bizarre and unimaginable firsts in a book that reads like a charcuterie board... bite-sized, meaty enough to fill in the blank spots in your history memory bank or launch you on a quest to learn even more. Learn more in a few pages than in an hour long documentary, this dictionary of disaster is right-sized doses of drama and it's all real. A great gift and a must for your coffee table."—*Chris Burrous, News Anchor, KTLA-5 Los Angeles*

"Dramatic accounts of the strange and bizarre moments of numerous forgotten tragedies. For lovers of quirky history, this is a fascinating glimpse into the *Forgotten Tragedies* of the past that cry out to be remembered. This book has something for everyone, the short stories are full of historical facts and drama without being too overwhelming. From the Great Molasses Flood to one of the first televised tragedies that brought a nation together, *Forgotten Tragedies* will leave you wanting more."—*Michelle Pennell, book critic*

"You don't have to be a 'Debbie Downer' to get something out of these twisted tales of misery and mayhem. They're bite-sized bits of history. An easy collection stories to pick up and hard to put down."—*Mai Do, former news anchor*

"Fascinating and compelling. A detailed walk through some of histories headliners that is thoroughly engaging. A page turner that in the end, left me wanting more."—*Toni Forster, Children's Author*

FORGOTTEN TRAGEDIES
Bob Dlugos

Moonshine Cove Publishing, LLC
Abbeville, South Carolina U.S.A.

ISBN: 978-1-945181-276
Library of Congress PCN: 2017918463
Copyright 2017 by Bob Dlugos

Dedication

For my wonderful wife Patty, for all of her precious love and support, and for my family and friends for all their encouragement

About the Author

I started this project after being inspired by another book I was writing, which also dealt with death. It occurred to me that in my lifetime there have been many tragedies to speak of, including the devastating losses of 9/11. But I began to wonder about the tragedies of the past that I had no knowledge of, that had impacted people as greatly as some of our recent tragedies have impacted us as a whole. I began to research the issue and found many tragedies that had eluded me in my lifetime, with details abounding on the internet. It seemed like it was time to chronicle these long-forgotten events, hence the title of this book. I sincerely hope the readers will honor the memories of those lost in these stories, and remember that life is not to be taken for granted. Live and love with great fervor, because tomorrow is not promised to anyone.

For more about the author, visit his Facebook page:

https://www.facebook.com/profile.php?id=100009593891816

Acknowledgment

Gene at Moonshine Cove Publishing for all his help and support, all the authors I borrowed from on the internet to make this book possible, my friends Chris, Steve, Toni, Michelle, and Mai for their support, my wife Patty for her unending love and support, my mother Martha for her love and support.

Contents

FORGOTTEN TRAGEDIES

Introduction

As a child I was always fascinated by the epic story of the *Titanic*; how a few simple mistakes could snowball into the loss of thousands of lives. The very idea of tragedy always sparked a curiosity in me, probably because these events highlight how truly unpredictable life can be.

Contained in these pages you will find tragedies great and small, all of which I found haunting and wanted to share. Some may be familiar, but many will be new to the reader, as they were new to me. From disasters on land to sea disasters even worse than the *Titanic* to stories which sadly reflect the tragedies of our own time, such as terror attacks. While many of these tragedies came about because of human error, some were manifested by mother nature, and the victims were simply in the wrong place at the wrong time, something which can happen to any of us. I think it's important that we keep these memories alive, not just for the lessons they can teach, but also that they may inspire us to value the everyday lives of people around us.

CLASSROOM TRAGEDIES

School Bomb Tragedy

It was an unthinkable tragedy. American school children targeted by a deadly mad bomber. It's a story straight out of a nightmare, but it actually happened.

The year was 1927. The place, Bath, Michigan. The Bath Consolidated School was a quiet, two-story building housing hundreds of students, many who would be the victims of the deadliest school attack in U.S. history.

The story really begins a year earlier. Fifty-five-year old Andrew Kehoe was a man known for his hot temper. He was the School Board Treasurer, and ran for Township Clerk in 1926. But Kehoe was defeated in a bitter race.

His wife was also struggling with tuberculosis, and the family farm was about to be foreclosed upon. It's believed this combination of setbacks motivated his deadly rage.

Kehoe slowly began to buy up parcels of dynamite sticks, which he hid under his house. He also began hiding them under the Bath Schoolhouse. For months he collected and stored the explosives. But because farmers occasionally used dynamite, no one suspected Kehoe, although neighbors dubbed him "the dynamite farmer" because of the occasional blasts which came from the property.

The tragedy began to unfold on May 16, 1927.

Sometime between then and the May 18, Kehoe's wife, who had recently been discharged from the hospital, was shot to death by Andrew. On May 18, Kehoe's house was destroyed in a massive explosion, which only left the chimney standing. As neighbors came to help, Kehoe drove away from the smoldering scene, telling rescuers "Boys, you're my friends. You'd better get out of here.

You better head down to the school." He left behind a sign on his fence, which read simply, "criminals are made, not born." An ominous ode to what was to come.

Classes had just begun at the Bath schoolhouse, with school kids beginning to crowd in at 8:30 for what was to be another ordinary day. But just minutes later, at 8:45, a small alarm clock hidden beneath the school's north wing went off. It was wired to hundreds of pounds of dynamite, causing a massive explosion which blew a corner of the schoolhouse to rubble. One witness, a first-grade teacher, said the air was full of flying children and desks. The north wing collapsed, bringing down part of the roof, leaving piles of splintered wood covering the agonizing moans of the injured and dying.

The death toll was staggering. 36 children died in the huge blast, along with two teachers. At least 58 others were injured. Parents came from all directions only to find the charred bodies of the small, helpless victims.

Amazingly, Kehoe, who had left the scene, returned a half-hour after the attack. He got the attention of the school superintendent, calling him to Kehoe's truck. Witnesses say the two began fighting over a rifle that Kehoe produced. Then, without warning, Andrew's truck, holding a cache of hidden dynamite, exploded. Four people, including the superintendent and Kehoe, died in the blast.

School Bomb Tragedy

In the aftermath, rescuers found another 500 pounds of dynamite that had not detonated, hidden underneath the south wing of the school. Terrifying to think that the country's greatest act of school terrorism could have been even deadlier.

The attack was front page news across the country for several day, until Charles Lindberg's famous crossing of the Atlantic ocean pushed the story out of the headlines, and slowly into obscurity. A park containing a spire from the schoolhouse now sits quietly where the tragedy unfolded, the only remnant of the old building left standing.

First U.S. School Shooting

Sadly, school shootings have become almost commonplace in America. From the horrors of Columbine High School, to the Virginia Tech massacre, thousands of students have died at the hands of gun violence. But you might be surprised to learn the first school shooting happened all the way back in 1764.

It's known as the Pontiac's Rebellion School Massacre. In 1763, war was declared by a group of Native American tribes from the Great Lakes area, the Illinois area, and Ohio area. Indians from the regions were dissatisfied with British postwar policies, after the French and Indian war. Warriors from numerous tribes began attacking British soldiers and settlers, trying to drive them away.

On July 26, 1764, four Lenape Indians entered a small log schoolhouse near the present-day city of Greencastle, Pennsylvania. Inside were schoolmaster Enoch Brown, and a group of young students. Brown pleaded with the warriors to spare the children, but instead they were shot, and scalped. The attackers then killed nine other children, also scalping them. Two children survived, and four others were kidnapped. But when the warriors returned to their village on the Muskingum River, the chief rebuked them as cowards for attacking children.

The gruesome attack caused lawmakers in Pennsylvania to re-introduce a bounty on Indians, which had previously been used during the French and Indian war. Settlers could collect 134 dollars for the scalp of an American Indian male over the age of ten.

Teacher Enoch Brown and the dead schoolchildren were buried in a common grave. In 1885, the area was named "Enoch Brown Park" and a large memorial was erected over the gravesite, to honor the victims of the first school shooting in U.S. history.

CSUF Shooting Massacre

Many remember the horrifying images of a sniper picking off students from atop a tower on the University of Texas campus in 1966. But few recall an eerily similar shooting rampage which happened on a quiet California college campus in the mid-1970's. An attack that left seven people dead.

July 12, 1976 began as an ordinary day on the campus of Cal State Fullerton. But a dangerous storm was brewing in the mind of janitor Edward Charles Allaway.

The 37-year-old was the custodian at the school library. He'd recently threatened his own wife with a knife and raped her, with the couple separating over the Memorial Day weekend. His wife filed for divorce shortly before the attack. Allaway also had a history of violence and mental instability, which including attacking a co- worker at a plant in Michigan.

At about 8:30 that morning, Charles arrived at work carrying a dangerous package, a .22 rifle he had bought at K-Mart. He slipped into a side door at the library, with blood on his mind. Once inside, he went down a stairwell and into the basement's media center. There, he fired his rifle, hitting photographer Paul Herzberg, killing him.

Equipment technician Bruce Jacobsen was also targeted and killed. Amazingly, secretary Karen Dwinell survived unharmed, as the shooter left seeking new targets.

Allaway fired his rifle down a long hallway where his bullets found two more victims: Professor Emeritus Seth Fessenden and graphic artist Frank Teplansky. The gunman then spotted two custodians, Debbie Paulsen and Donald Karges. Frightened, they ran down a windowless hallway, but couldn't escape the bullets which brought them both down.

The shooter then took a service elevator to the first floor of the library. There, he encountered a visiting high school student, who stood against a wall, terrified. For some reason, Allaway chose not to shoot, instead firing his rifle at the custodial supervisor Maynard Hoffman, who was shot as he tried to escape in an elevator. But before Charles could fatally shoot Hoffman, assistant librarian Stephen Becker smashed the gunman in the head with a metal plate. Library supervisor Donald Keran tried to wrestle the gun from Charles, but both he and Becker were wounded by stray gunshots. As Allaway fled through an emergency exit, Becker gave chase, but he was spotted by Allaway who shot him in the chest, killing Becker.

Finally, the shootings came to a halt, but only because the shooter ran out of bullets. Allaway ran from the library to his car, driving to the Anaheim hotel where his wife was employed. There, he called police. "I went berserk," he said on the phone, "and I committed some terrible act. I'd appreciate it if you people would come down and pick me up. I'm unarmed, and I'm giving myself up."

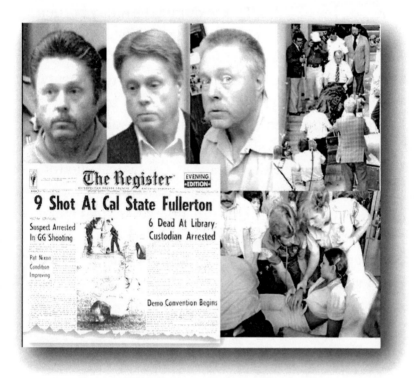

CSUF Shooting Massacre

Allaway was quickly arrested. But his trial would prove to be anything but quick. In his defense, the shooter said he was a victim of mental illness. He had tried to commit suicide in the past, and had even been treated with electric shock. His motive? Charles said his wife was being forced to do pornographic movies, which were being screened at the library before visiting hours.

While he was found guilty of six counts of first degree murder, and one count of second degree murder, the jury deadlocked during the sanity portion of the trial. A second phase of the trial determined he was not sane. Experts testified Allaway was a paranoid schizophrenic. He would be committed to a mental institution until being found sane. Guilty by reason of insanity. The shooter has applied several times for parole, but with no success.

Today, outside the library at Cal State Fullerton, stand seven trees in an area called the "memorial grove." Few students realize that the seven trees honor the victims of a forgotten shooting massacre, which happened right inside the very student library many use on a weekly basis.

School Bus Tragedy

It remains the worst school bus accident in U.S. history, the cloudy, cold day when 27 lives claimed in Prestonsburg, Kentucky, a now crash dubbed "The Big Sandy bus accident." It would have been much worse if not for the heroism of a number of students.

It was the cold, dreary morning of February 28, 1958. Driver John DeRossett began his usual route at 7 a.m. He would drive from Cow Creek to consolidated schools in Prestonsburg, collecting students along the way in the towns of Sugar Loaf and Emma.

The old bus number 27 he was driving had just been serviced, and didn't appear to have any problems that morning. DeRossett was on schedule, picking up children at their prescribed time. At about 8:10, at the mouth of Knotley Hollow just east of Prestonsburg, the driver stopped to pick up eight kids, including Ezelle Pennington. She recalled one of the little girls getting on with her, eight-year-old Rita Cheryl, was the "prettiest girl that ever was."

As they got on the bus, someone asked Ezelle's friend Joyce Matney why her grandfather's truck was down in a ditch. Sure enough, the pickup was stuck up to it's axles in mud, with a wrecker just arriving to pull out the trapped vehicle. As the bus driver pulled away, one student reportedly yelled that the bus would hit the tow truck. He couldn't have been more right.

The school bus slammed the back fender of the wrecker, turning hard to the left and toward the rushing river below. The bus slid down the bank and splashed down in the frigid, muddy water, bobbing briefly on the surface before beginning to sink.

One boy was able to kick open the emergency exit at the back of the bus. The strong current quickly pulled the bus away from the bank. Kids began jumping into the water and swimming away from the vehicle, but some recalling seeing young students in shock, holding each other. One boy escaped through an open window and pulled two younger children to safety. Ezelle scrambled over three seats to get to the emergency door where a small boy stood, frozen, refusing to jump into the water until his brother arrived. "I told him his brother was already out of the bus, so he jumped," she said. But it wasn't true. His brother didn't make it.

The wrecker driver and another man scrambled down the bank to begin pulling children from the icy water. Ezelle climbed the bank and as she looked back, she saw the bus almost completely submerged, little arms sticking out from the windows. One boy grabbed a small girl by the hair, but said the current was so strong the girl was ripped from his hands, leaving him with a handful of hair. The current moved the bus underwater about 250 feet from the crash site.

Investigators had a difficult time finding the bus, with Army engineers and volunteers not locating the battered and submerged vehicle for two days. When the bus was finally located, thousands of spectators lined the riverbank to see the bus pulled ashore by two bulldozers. The crowd gasped as the vehicle broke the surface, a girl's body hanging limply from the emergency door. Fifteen bodies were discovered in the mud-filled bus.

More bodies would be found in the river over the next few weeks. In all, 26 students and the bus driver were killed.

One father traveled 100 miles down the Big Sandy River in a boat, searching for his missing daughter. Her body was found by rescuers. Three families lost all of their children that day, and four other families lost two children. The victims ranged in age from 8 to 17.

Among the dead, little Rita Cheryl.

After all these years, the cause of the tragedy still remains a mystery. There were many conflicting witness accounts about what happened that blustery day.

Investigators say the bus driver had good visibility, and plenty of room to maneuver around the tow truck.

Questions about the brakes were never answered, because the front axle came off while the bus was being pulled from the water. Some suggested the driver had a heart attack, but an autopsy showed he drowned. No criminal charges or lawsuits were ever filed in the tragedy. An inquiry later cleared the bus driver of any wrongdoing.

School Bus Tragedy

School was suspended for weeks, and little Ezelle said when it was time to go back, she couldn't bring herself to get on the bus. It took several taxi rides for her to finally face her fear, and get back on board.

A stone monument was dedicated to the victims in

1994. It features 27 crosses for the 27 victims, and sits quietly atop a heart-shaped garden.

Deadly School Explosion Tragedy

It's the deadliest school disaster in U.S. history, but few remember the devastation caused by the New London School Texas explosion.

The tragedy happened on March 18, 1937. Close to 650 students and teachers were attending classes at the schoolhouse located in Rusk County. The school district was one of the richest in the country during the Great Depression, thanks to a huge oil find in 1930. The schoolhouse was built in 1932 at a cost of one-million dollars. It was a huge steel and concrete structure, and featured 72 gas heaters throughout the building, instead of the traditional boiler system. But the gas was not traditional natural gas; indeed, the school had canceled its' natural gas contract to save money, instead relying on excess gas piped in from the oil fields.

The odorless and colorless gas began to leak into the basement of the schoolhouse. Students had complained of headaches, but no one made the connection. On March 18, 1937, an instructor turned on an electric sander. It's believed the switch caused a spark that ignited the highly flammable gas-air mixture.

The explosion was fierce. Witnesses say the roof lifted from the building and crashed back down, the walls bulged, and the main wing of the school collapsed. A two-ton block of concrete was blown from the site through the air, crushing a car two miles away. The explosion was heard for miles. Within minutes, rescuers arrived from all over town, many digging through the rubble with their bare hands to try and find possible survivors. Roughnecks from the oil fields were released from their duties to help. They brought cutting torches and heavy equipment needed to clear the piles of concrete and steel. Soon the Texas National Guard was also called in to help. Even Boy Scouts took part in the rescue effort. A new hospital nearby was scheduled for its' grand opening the next day; the ceremony was canceled and the hospital opened to receive patients from the disaster.

It's believed as many as 319 people were killed in the huge blast, most of them students. However, we may never know the true number of victims, since many of the bodies that were initially dug out of the site were returned to their respective homes for burial. Many other bodies were burned beyond recognition. Amazingly, about 130 people escaped the blast with only minor injuries.

One of the first reporters to arrive on the scene was a young Walter Cronkite. He would later cover World War II, but said of the tragedy, "I did nothing in my studies nor in my life to prepare me for a story of the magnitude of that New London tragedy, nor has any story since that awful day equaled it." Oddly enough, one of the people who paid his respects after the disaster was German Chancellor Adolf Hitler. A copy of his telegram remains on display at the New London Museum.

Deadly School Explosion Tragedy

Investigators determined the connection between the residue gas line and the school was faulty. Because natural gas is invisible and odorless, the leak went unnoticed. Within weeks of the explosion, the Texas Legislature demanded that an odor-causing agent be added to natural gas, to help determine future leaks. The practice quickly spread worldwide. A lawsuit was brought against the school district and the oil company that supplied the gas, but the courts ruled neither could be held responsible. The school district superintendent was forced to resign, and even threatened with lynching. However, he too lost a family member in the blast, a young son.

A new school was built on the site of the demolished schoolhouse, and was known as London school until 1965, when the name was changed to West Rusk High School. The large granite memorial erected in 1939 now sits across Texas State Highway 42 from the school site, to commemorate the disaster. The tragedy has also been the subject of several documentaries, including *New London: the day the clock stood still* which featured the on-camera recollections of survivors of the blast, and *The Day a Generation Died*. Another documentary, *When Even Angels Wept* was released in 2009, and was a first-hand account of the disaster told by survivors and eyewitnesses.

A museum dedicated to the tragedy was opened in 1998, to remember the victims and the terrible aftermath of the horrible explosion.

MARITIME TRAGEDIES

Gustloff Ocean Liner Tragedy

The sinking of the *RMS Titanic* by an iceberg remains as the most memorable ocean liner tragedy of all time. More than 1,500 lives were lost in the chilly Atlantic when the ship went down. But amazingly, it's not the greatest loss of life in an ocean liner disaster.

The year was 1945. The world remained in the grip of a mighty World War, which would ultimately claim millions of lives. Among the victims would be the passengers of the *MV Wilheim Gustloff*, a huge ocean liner pressed into military service by the Germans. Its tragic sinking killed an estimated 9,400 people, or six times the loss of life on the fabled *Titanic*.

The *Gustloff* began life in 1937, as a cruise ship for the Nazis. It measured almost 700 feet in length.

Shipbuilders originally wanted to name it after Germany's leader, Adolf Hitler. But the ship was named the *Wilheim Gustloff* after a leader of the Nazi party, who was assassinated in 1936. Hitler made the decision while sitting next to *Gustloff's* wife at the funeral.

The huge ship was the flagship of the KDF cruise fleet, which stood for *"Kraft Durch Freude"* or "Strength through joy." It was meant to provide vacations to German workers, in an effort to make the Third Reich seem more acceptable around the world. The cruise ship Carried civilian passengers until war broke out in 1939.

She began her military career as a hospital ship that summer. The *Gustloff* would transport wounded German soldiers for the next year. Officials then decided to press the ship into action, as World War Two began to heat up. All medical equipment was removed from the liner, and it was painted a dull naval grey. The ship was mainly used as a floating barracks, housing about 1,000 U-boat trainees. Ironically, one of it's new duties was to provide soldiers as extras for a German movie being made about the *Titanic* disaster.

The *Gustloff* sat in silence for four years, until the advance of the Red army forced it back into service. The ship was to be used to evacuate German soldiers and refugees from both east and west Prussia. The passenger list cited 6,050 on board, but many civilians who had not been registered were also crammed onto the ocean liner hoping to escape the Russians. It's estimated about 10,500 people total were aboard, including more than 5,000 children. The overcrowding created uncomfortable conditions for the passengers, and many took off their life jackets.

The ship left Gotenhafen on January 30, 1945. It was accompanied by two torpedo boats, one of which broke down, leaving only a single military escort. A short time into the voyage, one of the four captains on board the *Gustloff* called for the ship to navigate shallow waters, to guard against submarine attack. But another captain decided the ship should go into deep water, that had already been swept for mines.

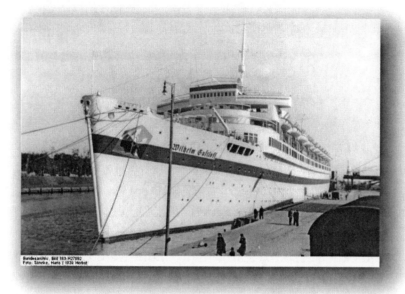

Gusstloff Ocean Liner Tragedy

Captain Friedrich Peterson also decided to activate the ship's red and green navigation lights, to avoid what he thought was an oncoming German minesweeper convoy. But the lights made the ocean liner much easier to spot for enemy forces. A Soviet submarine soon spotted the ship, which was helpless due to it's anti-aircraft guns freezing. The torpedo boat accompanying the *Gustloff* was blind to the presence of the submarine, with its sensor also frozen and inoperable. The ship was a sitting duck.

The Soviet sub stalked the ocean liner for two hours,

before taking action. Three torpedoes were fired, each slamming into the left side of the ship. The first caused the ship's watertight doors to seal, trapping off-duty crew members. The second destroyed a dry swimming pool in which people were sleeping, causing numerous casualties. The third torpedo then smashed into the engine room, cutting the ship's power and ability to send a message for help.

The freezing conditions continued to play havoc, as only one lifeboat could be lowered, the rest frozen in their davits. The frigid water claimed many lives as it rushed through the crippled ship. Others would try to escape the *Gustloff* by jumping into the ocean, only to quickly freeze to death. Many more were crushed in crowded stairwells as they attempted to flee. About forty minutes after the attack, the *Wilheim Gustloff* slipped below the frigid waves to the bottom of the ocean.

While German forces were able to rescue about 1,200 people, it's estimated the total loss of life was 9,343, including about 5,000 children.

Amazingly, all four captains survived the sinking.

Captain Petersen was never held accountable for his poor decisions, as the Nazi war machine collapsed later in 1945.

The *Wilhelm Gustloff* remains the largest loss of life resulting from a sinking in maritime history. The ship remains at the bottom of the ocean, classified as an official war grave.

Sultana Steamboat Tragedy

It was the worst maritime disaster in U.S. history, but it was swept aside by the torrent of stories regarding the assassination of President Lincoln, and the search and ultimate capture of shooter John Wilkes Booth. But the 1865 *Sultana* tragedy would take even more lives than the more-famous "*Titanic*" tragedy.

The *Sultana* was a side wheel Mississippi steamboat, originally meant to carry cotton. It also routinely carried troops during the U.S. Civil War between St. Louis and New Orleans. The ship was designed to carry a total of 376 passengers.

On April 13, 1865, the *Sultana* left St. Louis, bound for the Mardi Gras city. Captain J. Cass Mason was at the helm. The trip was uneventful until the paddle wheeler reached Vicksburg, Mississippi. There, Lieutenant Colonel Reuben Hatch offered the ship's captain a deal: the U.S. government would pay five dollars a soldier, and ten dollars per officer, to bring thousands of former prisoners of war from New Orleans to the north. He also promised a kickback to captain Mason, who took the bribe.

The *Sultana* limped into New Orleans with a leaky boiler. The ship's mechanic recommended cutting out a ruptured seam and replacing it, a job that would take several days. Captain Mason knew if he did the repair it would cost him his precious load of former prisoners, and decided instead to have a temporary repair made, which he thought would hold until further repairs could be procured.

The tragedy began to unfold on April 24th. Due to a clerical mix-up, the *Sultana* took on all of the former prisoners of war, an estimated 2,100. The men were packed like sardines in every available space on the boat. The overcrowding was so severe, sagging decks had to be supported with heavy wooden beams. The ship traveled for two days, stopping at Helena, Arkansas, where a photographer took a now-infamous picture of the grossly overcrowded ship.

Around two a.m. on April 27, the *Sultana* was about seven miles north of Memphis, Tennessee. Without warning, one of the ship's boilers exploded, with two more boilers also blowing a spilt seconds later. The blast destroyed a large section of the boat, hurling passengers into the water. The front section of the upper decks soon collapsed, falling onto the exposed furnace boxes and catching fire. Survivors, weakened from their prison stay, were too weak to swim for it, and many died clinging to each other in the inferno. Soon the entire upper portion of the *Sultana* was in flames.

The death toll may have been even higher if not for the crew of the steamer *Bostonia II*, which happened by about an hour after the catastrophe. Hundreds of survivors were helped out of the water and onto the ship. The remains of the *Sultana* drifted about six miles before it sank near Marion, Arkansas. While some died of burns or smoke inhalation, many died from drowning or hypothermia. About 700 survivors were taken to hospitals in Memphis, many with terrible burns. The death toll was estimated at 1,700, 200 more than the loss of life in the *Titanic* tragedy.

Sultana Steamboat Tragedy

Amazingly, no one was held accountable for the disaster. Army Captain Frederick Speed, who sent the former prisoners onboard, was charged with grossly overcrowding the *Sultana*, and found guilty. But he was later found innocent because while he approved the troop movement, he never actually put anyone on board.

Meanwhile, Colonel Hatch, who had concocted the plan to crowd the *Sultana* with passengers, quit the military and was no longer accountable to a military court. The ship's Captain Mason also escaped prosecution. It meant that no one was ever held accountable for the largest loss of life in U.S. maritime history.

Many of the dead were buried in nearby Memphis National Cemetery. Stone monuments to the victims were erected in several cities, including Memphis and Knoxville, Tennessee. The charred wreckage of the *Sultana* was found in 1982 about four miles from Memphis under a soybean field, about two miles from where the river runs today. The Mississippi has changed course numerous times so this should not be considered unusual.

Lancastria Tragedy

She was a British luxury liner capable of carrying 2,200 vacationers in the highest style. But the *RMS Lancastria* would face a tragic end due to the coming of World War Two, while trying to rescue thousands.

The ship was nearly 600 feet long, and was launched in 1920 under the name *Tyrrhenia* for the Anchor Line, a Subsidiary of the powerful Cunard Line. She carried thousands of passengers in three classes. But after passengers complained they couldn't pronounce the name of the ship, it was given the new name "*Lancastria*." The ocean liner sailed routinely from Liverpool to New York, and later was used as a cruise ship in the Mediterranean and Northern Europe.

The *Lancastria* proved to be a hero in 1932 when, on October 10 it saved the crew of the Belgian cargo ship *S.S. Scheldestad*, which was floundering in the Bay of Biscay. The heroic efforts would continue with the beginning of World War Two, when the *Lancastria* would be put into operation as a cargo ship, then re-assigned in April 1940 to carry troops. She was among the first ships to help evacuate troops from Norway.

The first sign of trouble for the *Lancastria* came during Operation Ariel, the evacuation of troops and British civilians from France following the Dunkirk evacuation. The ship was sunk off the French port of St. Nazaire, but was repairable. After a short overhaul, the ship left Liverpool on June 14, 1940. Captain Rudolph Sharp brought the liner to the mouth of the Loire, where she began picking up more troops, including RAF personnel, and civilian refugees. By June 17, the ship was bulging with thousands of people; some estimate as many as nine-thousand total. The ship was dangerously overloaded because Captain Sharp had been ordered by the Royal Navy to load as many people as possible, "without regard to the limits set down under international law."

The *Lancastria* attempted to leave when, during an air raid at 1:50 pm, a nearby ship, the *Oronsay*, was hit by a German bomb. The *Lancastria* was told to depart but was not given a destroyer escort. Captain Sharp chose to wait. Shortly before 4 p.m., another German air raid descended, and the *Lancastria* was hit by three different bombs, causing the ship to list first to starboard, then to port. The blasts were devastating, as 1400 tons of fuel oil leaked into the sea and were set afire. Passengers were thrown from the overloaded ship into the water, where many either drowned, choked on the oil, or were shot by strafing German aircraft. The end came quickly, as the *Lancastria* slipped under the water just twenty minutes after the deadly attack.

Nearby ships rushed to save the thousands left stranded in the water. Amazingly, close to 2500 people would be rescued, but the total loss of life was grim.

The official total would amount to 1,738 victims, but it's estimated as many as 5800 died in the tragedy, the largest loss of life in British maritime history. The loss of life was so great that at first the government suppressed the news of the disaster. But eventually the *New York Times* and other papers got wind of the sinking, and finally, the British *Daily Herald* ran the story on its' front page. As part of a government-ordered cover-up, survivors and rescuers alike were told not to discuss the tragedy.

Lancastria Tragedy

Captain Sharp survived the sinking; he would later die in 1942 when his new ship was torpedoed and sunk off West Africa.

The great ship now sits silently beneath the waves.

The British government has been asked to make the site a war grave, but has refused to do so, although it does qualify under the "Protection of Military Remains Act." Fourteen additional wrecks sunk at the Battle of Jutland were declared war graves in 2006, but not the *Lancastria*. The French placed an exclusion zone around the wreck in the early part of this century, and the British Ministry of Defense determined the move was enough to protect the wreckage.

Victims of the *Lancastria* are remembered every year with several parades and church services, both in London and in Edinburgh, Scotland. The tragedy is also remembered in a special stained glass window at the Church of St. Katherine Cree in London. A memorial was erected on the sea front at St. Nazaire in June of 1988, proclaiming "in proud memory of more than 4,000 who died", and also honoring those who helped rescue survivors and bury the victims.

General Slocum Tragedy

It's second only to 9/11 as the worst single loss of life in New York City history. But tragedy wouldn't strike from the sky, it would strike from the water.

The *General Slocum* was a paddlewheel ship built in Brooklyn in 1891. From the beginning it was plagued by problems. The boat was involved in a number of mishaps over the years, including collisions and running aground. Once, in June of 1902, the ship was grounded with 400 people aboard; it couldn't be moved until the next day, forcing the passengers to wait it out overnight on the cold paddle wheeler.

Tragedy struck on June 15 1904. The boat had been contracted for an excursion around New York City. On board were members of a church group from Manhattan. Its course was to sail up the East River and across Long Island Sound, to a picnic site in Eatons Neck Long Island.

Shortly after the ship left port, a fire broke out in the forward section, possibly caused by a discarded cigarette. A combination of straw, oily rags, and lamp oil fueled the flames. A 12-year old boy spotted the fire and tried to warn the captain, but nobody believed him.

The fire spread with alarming speed. When the crew

finally realized the danger, it manned the fire hoses; but the ship had been so poorly maintained by its' owners that the rotted fire hoses simply fell apart as soon as water was put through them. Even worse, the lifeboats were tied up and could not be accessed, plus the life jackets fell apart and were utterly worthless. Some mothers even put their children in the life vests and tossed them overboard to safety, only to see the vests give way and their children drown before their eyes. Many of the other victims simply didn't know how to swim, and were swallowed by the dark, murky water.

Rather than trying to stop the ship at a nearby landing, or even running the ship aground, Captain William Van Schaick chose to continue his course. But investigators say he actually fanned the flames by sailing into headwinds. The fire began to consume the ship, and many died when the floors of the boat collapsed. Some were even killed by the paddle wheel on the side of the boat as they floundered in the water.

The *General Slocum* finally sank in shallow water just off the Bronx shore at North Brother Island. It's estimated 1,021 people died in the tragedy, with only 321 survivors reported. Captain Van Schaick lost an eye to the fire. He would later say he didn't want to run the ship aground because he was afraid nearly homes and businesses would be set ablaze. Eight people would be indicted for the tragedy, including the Captain. However, only Captain Van Schaick would be convicted, on charges of criminal negligence. The charge stemmed from the Captain's reluctance to maintain proper emergency equipment, and for not scheduling proper fire drills. He served three and a half years before a Presidential pardon freed him on Christmas day, 1912. The disaster motivated both federal and state regulators to improve the emergency equipment supplied on passenger ships. The sunken remains of the *General Slocum* were later salvaged and turned into a barge, which would later sink in the Atlantic while carrying a load of coal.

General Slocum Tragedy

In 1906, a memorial fountain was placed at Tompkins Square Park on Manhattan. It reads "They are Earth's purest children, young and fair." An annual memorial ceremony is also held at a historical market at

Lutheran All Faiths Cemetery in Queens, to honor those who died in the tragedy.

Fire Tragedies

Chicago Theater Fire Tragedy

It's often been said that one should not yell "fire" in a crowded theater, because it might induce panic. It is certain that a real fire in a crowded theater can be disastrous, and one fire in particular in a Chicago theater at the turn of the century led to the single-deadliest building fire prior to 9/11 in U.S. history.

The venue was the Iroquois Theater on West Randolph street. It opened in November 1903 after numerous delays; but once open, theater critics applauded the new venue. The Iroquois was meant to attract women on day trips to Chicago, with it's proximity to the police- patrolled Loop Shopping District. The theater could seat more than 1,600 people on three levels, with everyone using the same entrance. The common stairwell was against Chicago fire ordinances, but the designers said it was necessary to allow patrons to see and be seen regardless of the price of their seats. The decision would prove deadly.

Amazingly, the theater was promoted as being "absolutely fireproof" in playbills. But a Chicago Fire Captain who toured the facility noted a lack of sprinklers, fire alarms, water connections, or telephones to call for help. The only fire equipment on site were six dry chemical fire extinguishers, which came in tube form. The instructions called for the user to hurl the canisters into the fire to squelch it.

On December 30, 1903, a Wednesday matinee performance of the popular musical *Mr. Bluebeard* was playing. The sellout crowd also included hundreds of standing room only tickets. It's estimated about 2,100 of the patrons were children. The theater was so crowded that some people sat in the aisles, blocking escape routes.

It was at the beginning of the second act about 3:15, when a possible short circuit caused a light to spark high above the stage, igniting a curtain. A stagehand tried to throw the fire extinguishers at the flames, but the canisters fell helplessly to the ground. The flames quickly spread to the gallery high above the stage which housed the painted canvas scenery backgrounds. A stage manager tried to lower the asbestos fire curtain, but it got stuck.

The star of the show immediately ran on stage to try and calm the crowd, pleading with patrons not to panic even as flaming debris fell around him. The spectators began to flee the burning theater, but some found they could not open the fire doors, which had a newly-designed and difficult unlocking mechanism. Only a few of the fire doors could actually be opened, the rest held fast against the crush of theater-goers frantically trying to escape.

Many died in the dead ends provided by the fire doors.

As the performers escaped from the backstage area, open doors allowed wind to rush in and fuel the growing flames. Many attempted to get out using a door that opened inwards, and jammed by the crush of the performers. They would have died there if not for a passing railroad agent who saw what was happening, and unfastened the hinges from the outside. The massive freight doors were also opened, which brought in a cyclonic blast of air, creating an enormous fireball which incinerated the front seats, including those still trapped there. Those in the higher levels tried escaping down the stairways, but were trapped by iron grates which barred the openings. It was later determined most of the casualties came from the stairways, where hundreds were found crushed, or suffocated from the smoke. Some were able to make it to unfinished fire escapes, and jumped to their deaths. A few were able to crawl from the roof to a nearby rooftop, where a ladder had been extended across for rescue.

By the time the fire department arrived, the tragedy was already in full force. Once the flames were extinguished, rescuers entered the theater to find bodies stacked ten high. An estimated 575 people died in the fire, with at least another 30 dying later from their injuries. The Mayor ordered all theaters in Chicago closed for six weeks after the tragedy, to investigate numerous charges. Some even claimed fire inspectors had been bribed with free tickets, to overlook code violations.

Chicago Theater Tragedy

Sadly, while several people were charged with crimes, including the theater manager, the only person who would ever be convicted in the Iroquois Theater Fire was a local tavern keeper, charged with grave robbing.

While the fire destroyed the inside of the building, the structure was intact, and it was rebuilt as the Colonial Theater. That was demolished to make way for the Oriental Theater, which still stands today. Some have suggested it is haunted by the ghosts of the victims of the Iroquois fire, which claimed an estimated 602 people, although most believe the death toll was higher.

Circus Fire Tragedy

The circus. For generations, a day of fun for the entire family with clowns, wild animals, and trapeze artists entertaining happy children and parents alike. But the history of the circus also has a tragic side, the day sometimes known as "the day the clowns cried."

It was July 6, 1944 in Hartford, Connecticut, at the afternoon performance of the best known circus in the world, Ringling Brothers and Barnum & Bailey. The show was held in a huge tent known simply as "the big top." So big it could seat about 9,000 people. Oddly, at the time the tents were waterproofed by coating them with paraffin wax and gasoline. A mixture which would have tragic consequences.

The crowd that day was huge; an estimated 7,000, mostly made up of women and children. The show was in full stride when a small flame was seen on the southwest sidewall of the tent, during the performance of the famous aerialists the "Great Wallendas." As the smoke began to rise, Ringmaster Fred Bradna recognized the danger, and told the band to play "The Stars and Stripes Forever," a tune which traditionally was used as a distress signal for all circus personnel. As the fire began to grow, the Ringmaster called into his microphone for calm and an orderly exit from the tent.

But the fire caused a power failure, and he couldn't be heard. As the canvas burned ever brighter, frightened spectators began to panic, pushing and trampling their way out of the now fully- engulfed circus tent. Witnesses say many victims simply ran in circles trying to find loved ones, while others escaped but ran back into the inferno searching for family members. Others remained seated, sure the fire would be put out eventually, and died in their seats.

The big top, treated with paraffin and gasoline, was a perfect host for the flames, which spread rapidly. Along with the smoke and fire, many people were injured by the hot melting wax pouring down from above. Witnesses said the tent came down in just eight minutes, trapping hundreds of spectators inside.

The death toll was staggering. It's estimated at 168 people, although the numbers included body parts of victims so badly burned they were not recognizable.

Experts now believe the death toll was even higher, because the fire was so hot it may have cremated some of the victims. Many of the dead were found in piles, although a few people somehow survived at the bottom of the piles, protected from the flames by the bodies above them. At least 700 people were injured; although that number is also in dispute, because witnesses reported dozens of injured people leaving the burning tent in shock, only to return to their homes without seeking treatment. Also, free tickets had been handed out that day in town, and a true count of the crowd was never made.

Amazingly, none of the animals were harmed, except for some minor burns suffered by the lions, who were also performing at the time of the fire.

Circus Fire Tragedy

Decades later, the cause of the deadly circus fire remains unsolved. Investigators originally believed a lit cigarette may have sparked the blaze. However, a young circus worker named Robert Segee reportedly confessed to starting the blaze, while being investigated on other arson charges. Investigators say Segee knew intimate details of the fire that only the real arsonist would have known, such as the fact that two smaller fires were reported at the circus prior to the tragedy. The suspect claimed he had a nightmare of an Indian riding on a flaming horse who told him to set fires, and that he blacked out, regaining consciousness only as the tent was burning. One investigator said Segee fit the "textbook description of a serial arsonist." Robert later recanted his confession, and was never tried for the crime. He was later convicted of arson in Ohio, and sentenced to forty years in prison.

Charges of involuntary manslaughter were brought against five Ringling Brothers employees, four of whom were convicted, but later pardoned. The circus ended up paying out about five million dollars in damages to 600 victims and families who had filed claims. One of the most famous victims of the fire is a little girl, about age five, who was dubbed "little miss 1565," which was the number assigned to her at the morgue.

Though her face was burned on one side, her features were easily recognizable, but no one claimed her body, despite massive publicity and showings of her photo in magazines around the country. She was later buried without a name in Hartford's Northwood Cemetery, where a memorial to the victims also stands.

A photo of the tragedy appeared in many newspapers the next day. It featured the famous clown Emmett Kelly holding a water bucket. It was dubbed "the day the clown cried."

Cocoanut Grove Fire Tragedy

It was the worst nightclub fire in the history of the U.S. A sudden and tragic blaze so horrific, it would take the lives of hundreds of people simply out for a night on the town. And as with many such tragedies, much of it could have been prevented.

The Cocoanut Grove was a popular destination for those looking for a little fun on a Boston night. It sported a tropical theme, complete with bamboo, fake palms, and even a removable roof for summer nights. It also featured a revolving front door. The Grove had served as a speakeasy during the prohibition days, and was a hangout for bootleggers, but had become a favorite place to hang out and forget the sorrows of World War I.

The club was owned by Barney Welansky, a man believed to have mob ties. He also didn't care about fire safety, blocking exits so customers wouldn't sneak out without paying their tab. One fire exit had even bricked up. The decision would prove tragic.

It was a festive Thanksgiving weekend when all hell broke loose. On November 28, 1942, over a thousand people crammed the nightclub, which was meant to hold less than half that amount. The party was in full swing, with the orchestra just beginning the evening show.

Shortly after ten p.m., a patron unscrewed a light bulb, possibly to get more privacy for him and his girl. Sixteen-year old busboy Stanley Tomaszewski lit a match to try and find the discarded lightbulb in the darkness. Whether it was his match or something else that ignited the flames, we may never know. But in an instant, the fake palm fronds began to burn. The fire spread quickly, climbing the wall decorations and onto the ceiling, which was covered in cloth draperies. The flames raced up the stairwell to the main level. Patrons making their way up the stairs had their hair singed by the blaze. A fireball burst across the dance floor and through the Caricature Bar, then down a corridor to the Broadway Lounge.

Within five minutes, the entire nightclub was ablaze.

Panicked patrons raced to the front door, desperate to escape.

There they met a bottleneck of people, made worse by the fact that the front door was a revolving door. Bodies began to pile up around the door, jamming it. Other escape routes were hampered by inward-opening doors, and boarded windows. Several members of the orchestra died, including musical director Bernie Fazioli. Victims were killed not only by the flames, but by breathing in the thick toxic smoke. Some were even found still sitting with drinks in hand, perishing too quickly to even move.

Rescuers from nearby bars raced to help, including

soldiers and sailors on leave from the war. Firefighters burned their hands trying to remove the burning bodies. As the night wore on, the temperature dropped, causing fire hoses to freeze to the cobblestone road. Newspaper trucks were employed as makeshift ambulances to usher out the wounded.

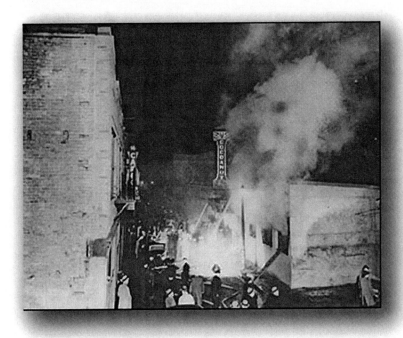

Cocoanut Grove Tragedy

One tragic escape involved Coast Guard member, Clifford Johnson. Thinking his date was still caught in the fire, he went back into the flaming nightclub three times, receiving third-degree burns over 55% of his body.

Amazingly, he survived his ordeal and married his nurse. But his life took a final tragic turn when he died 14 years later in another fire that resulted from a car crash.

In the end, a total of 492 people lost their lives in the Cocoanut Grove disaster. The official verdict was that the fire was of "unknown origin." Owner Barney Welansky was convicted of manslaughter for his part in the deadly blaze, and was sentenced to 15 years. He served four before being pardoned, and died of cancer a short time later.

The tragedy would create new safety standards for clubs, including visible exit signs and a ban on exit doors that swung inward. Amazingly, new techniques for caring for burn victims were discovered, with the use of the new drug penicillin proving very helpful in treating the survivors.

The tragedy shocked the nation, and accounts of the disaster even pushed news about World War II to the back pages.

The destroyed building was torn down shortly after the investigation was complete. For decades after the fire, the land was used as a parking lot. Much of the footprint of the old Cocoanut Grove now sits beneath the Revere Hotel. A surviving section of the street was renamed Cocoanut Grove Lane in 2013, in honor of the victims. A bronze plaque also sits at the site, in mute testimony to the great tragedy.

Peshtigo Fire Tragedy

Many believe the great Chicago fire of 1871 was the worst in American history, thanks to the tales of Mrs. O'Leary's cow, and the amount of national coverage the fire got in newspapers. But amazingly, the worst wildfire in U.S. history happened the very same day, and has been lost to time.

It's known as the "Peshtigo Firestorm of 1871." Peshtigo was a small frontier town with a population of about 1700 people. It was located in Wisconsin, and the area was surrounded by forests of Oak, Maple, pine, and other popular woods. The area even boasted the country's largest wood factory in the country, serving the construction needs of several states.

But the area was also a power keg waiting to explode. Farmers were known to use "slash and burn" methods to clear their lands, and rail workers were known to leave cut brush by the railroad tracks, where passing trains would often ignite the piles. Add to this a long and dry summer drought, and the conditions were ripe for tragedy.

It began on October 8. A storm system with heavy winds invaded the area, causing at least one small railroad brush fire to spread. One witness recalled "the menacing crimson reflection on the western sky was rapidly increasing in size and intensity... the strange and terrible noise of fire." The air began to clog with smoke and ash.

The winds fanning the fire caused it to roar into blazing life, creating a wall of flame some estimated to be as high as a mile, and five miles across. The fire raced along at an estimated 100 miles and hour, devouring everything in it's path. The flames were so intense they jumped the waters of the Peshtigo river. Several residents said a fire tornado tossed railroad cars and even houses into the air.

Some died when they tried to escape by entering the water, later drowning or dying from hypothermia. One tale of survival says a group of families fled to a church in nearby Robinsonville. There they prayed to the Virgin Mary for help, and although the area was consumed by fire, the little church remained standing and everyone inside was safe. The smoke from the fire was so dense it even caused a three-masted schooner to crash offshore, although the crew was rescued.

By sunrise the next day, the Peshtigo fire had claimed an area twice the size of Rhode Island. The devastation was that of a nuclear bomb, with the fire destroying everything in it's path. The death toll was staggering. It's estimated between 1,200 and 2,500 people were killed. The numbers are based in part on a report to the Wisconsin Legislature, which listed close to 1,200 people missing and presumed dead in the area. The fire scorched 1.2 million acres, at a cost of about 170 million dollars, the same as the great Chicago fire. Along with Peshtigo, 16 other towns were laid waste, before changing weather and firefighting efforts reduced the blaze to ashes.

Peshtigo Fire Tragedy

Today, Peshtigo is home to the Peshtigo Fire Museum, located in a former church. It hosts a small collection of artifacts from the fire, and stories from witnesses to the tragedy. Next to the museum is the Peshtigo Fire Cemetery, where a solemn memorial stands in dedication to the victims. More than 350 people lie buried in a mass grave, their identities known only to history.

Railway Tragedies

The Great Train Crash Tragedy

In Philadelphia, it was known as "The Picnic Train Tragedy," and in Montgomery County, Pennsylvania, "The Camp Hill Disaster." Either way, it was the deadliest train crash up to that time, and a defining moment in the 19 century.

The accident happened July 17, 1856, five years before the beginning of the Civil War. A train operated by the North Pennsylvania Railroad, and christened "the Picnic Special," had been hired by St. Michael's Church in Philadelphia to send Sunday School kids on a picnic in a sprawling grove known as Shaeff's Woods. The train was carrying as many as 1500 people, according to estimates.

Because of the large crowd, the train left its station at Master Street and Germantown Avenue 23 minutes late, at 5:10 a.m. The locomotive was named "Shakamaxon" and was engineered by operator Henry Harris.

Meanwhile another train, the "Aramingo," waited at the station in Wissahickon for the party train to pass.

Normally, a conductor could use a telegraph to find out the status of the train which would be sharing a single track line. But sadly, in this case the telegraph remained silent, and Aramingo conductor William Vanstavoren, after waiting the customary 15 minutes, pulled out of the station.

The engineer of the Shakamaxon was aware that he was behind schedule, but felt he could make up lost time, and that the two engines could use the siding at Edge Hill to safely pass each other. His calculations were wrong.

As the Shakamaxon neared a blind hill just past Camp Hill Station, it blew it's whistle to let the oncoming train know it was coming. But while the whistle was heard by the Aramingo, it didn't know where the other train was until they both rounded a curve, and suddenly caught sight of each other. The brakes were applied, but it was too late.

At 6:18 a.m., the two huge trains collided. The head-on impact of the two boilers created an explosion which was heard five miles away. The three wooden cars of the picnic train were decimated, and quickly caught fire as they lay derailed on their sides. Frantic women and children screamed as they tried to escape the flaming cars. Rescuers came from all around to try and help, but the heat of the burning wreckage was so intense it drove them back.

A bucket brigade was quickly established to a nearby stream. But the effort proved futile. Finally, a fire truck from The Congress Engine and Hose Company arrived, and was able to quickly put out the fire. As the tragic news reached the town of Wissahickon, men rushed from the factories to help. But the flames roasted alive many who were trapped in the burning passenger cars.

Many bodies were so badly burned they could not be identified. The death toll fell somewhere between 59 and 67, with more than 100 people injured. Sadly, most of the victims were children. The engineer of the picnic special also died, but the conductor of the Aramingo, William Vanstavoren, escaped uninjured. He always felt responsible for the crash. After he returned home to Philadelphia and officially reported the accident, he went home and drank arsenic. Sadly, he was later absolved of any blame; the dead engineer of the Shakamaxon was found guilty of gross carelessness.

One woman would be remembered as the heroine of the tragedy. Mary Johnson Ambler, who lived near the crash site, quickly gathered up first-aid materials and ran the two miles to the accident scene. There, she cared for the injured and dying. After her death in 1868, the nearby railroad station was renamed in her honor; and eventually the town of Wissahickon was named Ambler, as a tribute to her heroism.

The North Pennsylvania Railroad went to great lengths to help survivors and the families of the victims, issuing shares of company stock which would later prove quite valuable. Several changes were also put into effect, including the routine use of the telegraph to notify stations of late trains. Another case of a major policy change coming too little too late, to save the victims of a major tragedy.

Train Bridge Tragedy

It was an unthinkable tragedy. A train passing over a bridge during a violent storm, suddenly being slammed by a huge wave of water. It sounds like the stuff of some recent disaster movie special effects, but it actually happened.

The date was August 7, 1904. More than 100 passengers were on board the Number 11 Missouri Pacific Flyer, traveling from Denver to St. Louis for the World's Fair. Engineer Charles Hinman received a thunderstorm warning, and drove the train cautiously at about ten miles an hour, keeping an eye out for wash outs.

The engine of the train safely crossed the Dry Creek Arroyo Bridge about eight miles north of Pueblo, Colorado, when tragedy struck. A tremendous, rushing wall of water slammed into the portion of the train still on the bridge. It broke the coupling to the rear two passenger cars, and dragged the engine back into the river. A porter on one of the remaining passenger cars quickly pulled the emergency air brake, and the front car screeched to a stop, with about four feet of the car hanging over the now-demolished bridge. The other cars were thrown violently into the surging water.

Only three passengers and one fireman officially

escaped the deadly accident; some newspapers reported another 29 people in the back cars were also saved, but the accounts vary. The official death toll stands at 97, with at least 14 of the bodies never to be found.

Train Bridge Tragedy

The engine was discovered submerged near the bridge, while the chair car was found almost a mile downstream. Bodies began washing up, and were found as far as four miles down the river. The first rescue trains arrived about four hours after the catastrophe.

Bloodhounds were used to try and find survivors, but

were pulled back because of quicksand.

Amazingly, crews set to work rebuilding the bridge, and it was operational within 24 hours of the accident.

The bridge was rebuilt around the remains of the engine which had crashed below. A simple wooden sign now marks the site of the bizarre tragedy, which was the worst train tragedy of the time.

Circus Train Tragedy

There is nothing quite like a circus. Especially in the days of the early 1900s, when the show filled with bubbly clowns, ferocious animals, and amazing spectacles which would travel from city to city via the rails. But sadly, one of the great train wrecks in U.S. history would involve one of these colorful traveling showcases.

It began in the early morning hours of June 22, 1918, near the town of Hammond, Indiana. Four hundred performers and roustabouts of the Hagenbeck-Wallace circus were traveling to their next destination on a slow-moving, 26-car train. Following behind was a faster- moving Michigan Central Railroad troop train with 20 empty Pullman cars. The engineer of that train, Alonzo Sargent, was aware of the slower train ahead of him. He was a very experienced driver, with about 28 years in the cab. In later testimony, Sargent would say he had almost no sleep in the 24 hours prior to the crash, and had consumed two heavy meals, knowing he wouldn't be able to eat for quite a while.

Whether it was the rich food or the lack of sleep, at about 4 a.m. the engineer nodded off at the controls. He missed at least two automatic signals and warnings posted by the brakeman of the circus train, which had made an emergency stop about six miles east of Hammond, to check on one of the flatcars. Without warning, the second train slammed into the back of the circus train at about 35 miles an hour. It plowed through the caboose and into the four wooden sleeping cars, causing a large fire. Many of the victims burned to death in the flammable passenger cars. All told, 86 people lost their lives in the crash, including well-known acts "the great Dierckx Brothers" and Jennie Ward Todd of "The Flying Wards." In addition, 127 people were injured in the rear-end crash.

Engineer Sargent survived the disaster, and was one of dozens who helped the survivors escape the twisted wreckage. He was arrested at the site, and later brought before an investigation by the joint Interstate Commerce Commission and the Indiana Public Service Commission. In his testimony, Sargent said he awoke just seconds before the crash to see the red tail lights of the circus train; he slammed on the brakes while his fireman ran to safety. Sargent and his fireman were both criminally charged, but a Lake County, Indiana jury deadlocked on the charges, and a mistrial was declared. Prosecutors decided not to re-try the case. A report on the crash was critical of the old wooden cars, and suggested the oil lamps on board probably started the fire after the collision.

Circus Train Tragedy

Five days after the crash, most of the bodies lay burned beyond recognition. They were buried in Woodlawn Cemetery in Forest Park, Illinois, in a plot which purchased by the Showman's League of America just a few months earlier. The names of most of the circus workers were unknown because the bodies could not be identified; most of the graves still carry the monikers "unknown male" or "unknown female." One grave is marked "Smiley", one "Baldy", and another "Four-Horse Driver". Surrounding the section are statues of elephants in a mourning posture, to symbolize the loss of the circus performers in the tragedy

The Great Train Wreck

It's been called "The great train wreck of 1918." Yet it was so long ago, few know of this deadly crash, the worst in U.S. history.

It happened on July 9, in Nashville, Tennessee. The two trains involved were the Number Four, which was departing Nashville for Memphis, and the Number One, headed in the opposite direction. Both trains were operated by the Nashville, Chattanooga and St. Louis Railway. Number Four had six wooden coaches, along with two baggage and mail cars. Number One also had six wooden coaches, but contained two all-steel Pullman sleeping cars.

Number One was running more than a half-hour behind schedule. As per the track rules of the day, the inbound train had the right of way. Railroad dispatch radioed Number Four to stop in the double-track section to let Number One pass. As train Number Four hit the double-track section, the conductor heard the sound of a passing engine, and assumed it was Number One, giving Number Four the right to get back on the single track. It was a deadly mistake.

As the Number Four train approached Shops Junction, the tower operator noted there was no entry in his log that the Number One had passed. Panicked, he telegraphed the dispatcher, who wired back "can you stop him?" Johnson sounded the emergency whistle, but no one on Number Four heard it.

About 7:20 a.m. the two trains collided at Dutchman's Grade near White Bridge road. Both trains were traveling at speeds over 50 miles per hour when the crash happened. The massive head-on collision could be heard for two miles. The two engines were reduced to unrecognizable masses of twisted iron and steel. Many of the wooden cars were crushed or thrown sideways off the track, splintered by the impact.

Thousands came from around the area to help with the wounded survivors. What they found were dozens of bodies in the tangled aftermath of the crash. One account says as many as 50,000 people came to the scene to either help, or be spectators to the gruesome sight.

The official death toll was listed as 101, although some reports have it as high as 121. Another 171 were injured in the crash. Many of the victims were African-American laborers from Arkansas and Memphis, coming to work at the gunpowder plant outside of Nashville.

The Interstate Commerce Commission cited a combination of operating practices, human error and lax enforcement of operating rules as the cause of the deadly collision. The wreck was also the driving force behind many railroads switching to all-steel passenger cars.

The Great Train Wreck

Sadly, it was to have been the last trip before retirement, for the engineer of the Number One train. The crash was memorialized in the 1980 song "The great Nashville railroad disaster" by singer David Allan Coe. A mournful reminder of a very tragic day.

Avalanche Train Tragedy

It's one of the great dangers of snow country. Each year dozens of people around the world are killed by avalanches. Tons of snow sent sliding down mountainsides, mowing down everything in it's path. But one avalanche did the unthinkable, causing a deadly train wreck.

The tragedy began to unfold on February 23, 1910, when heavy snow caused a snow delay at the east Cascade Mountain town of Leavenworth, Washington. Passenger train number 25 was eventually able to move through a tunnel near Wellington, but was held near the town due to the heavy snowfall, below Windy Mountain. The train was stuck for six days as crews tried unsuccessfully to clear the tracks.

Then on February 28, the weather turned to rain with thunder and lightning. The thunder shook the snow-capped mountain, causing small avalanches, but no one was injured. But this was just the prelude to tragedy.

In the early morning hours of March 1, there was another rumble from the electrical storm. But it wasn't thunder. Railroad employee Charles Andrews was walking toward a bunkhouse when he heard a low, trembling sound, and turned to see the side of the mountain coming down. In a statement, Andrews later described it as: "White Death moving down the mountainside above the trains. Relentlessly it advanced, exploding, roaring, rumbling, grinding, snapping — a crescendo of sound that might have been the crashing of ten thousand freight trains. It descended to the ledge where the side tracks lay, picked up cars and equipment as though they were so many snow-draped toys, and swallowing them up, disappeared like a white, broad monster into the ravine below."

Avalanche Train Tragedy

Victims inside the train say they saw the lightning flashes, then heard an ominous low roaring sound headed straight for the train cars. Passengers were lifted and tossed inside the passenger coaches, which were tumbled hundreds of feet down the side of a ravine, and buried under 40 feet of snow. Andrews and a number of witnesses immediately sprang to life, hustling down to the smashed trains to begin digging out survivors. 23 people made it out alive. The bodies of the remaining victims were taken by toboggan to other trains, which carried the remains to Everett and Seattle. In all, 96 people died in the avalanche, including 35 passengers and 58 railroad employees on board. Three other employees sleeping in a nearby cabin were also killed in the crushing snow.

Investigators later determined that while the immediate cause of the avalanche was due to rain and thunder, fires caused by steam locomotive sparks led to the clear cutting of forest above the spot where the deadly accident occurred. It created a natural slide path for the avalanche. Because the small town of Wellington became known for the crash, city leaders renamed the town Tye to avoid further bad publicity. It took about three weeks to fix the mangled railroad tracks. By 1913, snow sheds had been constructed along the route, to protect trains from snow slides.

The accident remains the worst loss of life from an avalanche in history.

Flooding Tragedies

Molasses Flood Tragedy

Flooding is one of nature's deadliest disasters.

Floodwaters claim hundreds of lives every year. But one killer flood was not the result of heavy rains or mud, but a river of molasses. It's known as the "Great Molasses Flood."

The time was January 15, 1919. The Purity Distilling Company in Boston, owned by the United States Industrial Alcohol Company, had built an enormous tank to house it's molasses. At 50 feet tall and 90 feet across, the enormous structure held a staggering two and a half million gallons of the sticky sweet substance. The company used it to make alcohol for both drinking and industrial use.

Shortly after noon, something went tragically wrong.

Rivets holding together the massive five-story tank began to pop. Witnesses said it sounded like gunfire. As the steel ripped open, the molasses was freed in a 15-foot wall of sticky liquid. A total of 26-million pounds moved in a wave down a Boston street, at an estimated 35 miles per hour. More than enough force to shatter buildings, snap the support girders from an elevated train track, and smash nearby homes. The local firehouse was pushed over and destroyed. Railroad freight cars were dislodged from their tracks and swept away. For the people unlucky enough to be caught in the advancing wave of molasses, well, they didn't stand a chance. Victims were either knocked down and crushed by the wall of thick liquid and debris, or they simply drowned in the oozy mess. People, horses and dogs caught in the syrup struggled to escape, only sinking further. Rescuers had to slog through the waist-deep goo to try and help the survivors. 21 people died in the molasses flood, and another 150 were injured.

Molasses Flood Tragedy

The troubles didn't end there. Cleaning up the sticky mess proved to be a formidable task. The high-water mark of the flood rose 15 feet off the ground. Firefighters hoped to be able to hose off the molasses stuck to roads and buildings, but had no luck. Eventually, someone realized saltwater would cut through the hardened substance, allowing it to disappear down the city's gutters. The cleanup took several weeks and an estimated 80,000 man hours.

Initially, the company blamed a saboteur for the destructive flood. But investigators soon learned the cause of the tragedy was shoddy workmanship on the huge holding tank. The walls were reportedly too thin to hold back the millions of gallons, and the steel used was too brittle to withstand the pressure. It was also believed the molasses had fermented, producing gas which raised the pressure inside the cylinder.

The disaster produced more than 100 lawsuits against the United States Industrial Alcohol Company. It was determined the tank had not been built properly, with officials ignoring the numerous leaks of the tank over the years. As a result, Industrial Alcohol was forced to pay nearly one-million dollars in claims, a hearty sum for 1919, but little compensation for such an unusual and bizarre disaster.

London Beer Flood Tragedy

It was an English tragedy that bore resemblance to the Great Molasses Flood in the U.S. But the culprit this time was beer- and lots of it.

The date was October 17, 1814. Nestled among the homes and tenements of the poor was a small brewery known as Meux and Company in the parish of St. Giles, London. The area was ripe with crime and prostitution.

Whole families were known to live in the basements of those crumbling dwellings. This would prove unfortunate for many of the occupants.

The Meux brewery held within its walls a 22-foot high wooden fermentation tank, holding thousands of gallons of brown porter ale. The tank was tethered together by large iron rings. Without warning, one of those rings snapped, and the huge beer vat broke open, sending out a cascade of over 135,000 gallons of beer. The back wall of the brewery fell open, and the force of the rupture impacted several nearby vats, causing them to fail as well. In an instant, a torrent of more than 323,000 gallons of beer escaped and was on the move.

The huge 15-foot high wave of beer moved through the town. It first destroyed two homes, knocking down the old brick as if it were paper. Next to go was the Tavistock Arms pub, which crumbled, killing a teenaged girl who was working at the time. The wave of beer swamped nearby streets, and flooded basements full of people. One group was gathered for a wake to mourn the loss of a four-year-old boy the day before. Four of them were trapped in the basement flood and drowned. Other victims of the foamy sea of suds included a mother and daughter who were taking tea at the time. At least eight people are known to have died in the tragedy.

Amazingly, in the midst of the tragedy, people began to scoop up the "free beer" in whatever containers they could find handy. There was even a rumor that a ninth victim died due to alcohol poisoning, from drinking too much of the beer.

The stench would linger in the town for months.

While some tried to rebuild, others put their dead loved ones on display for money. At one home, the macabre exhibition proved so popular, that the weight of the visitors caused the floor to collapse into the beer-flooded basement.

Although the brewery was taken to court over the incident, no one was found responsible, as the judge ruled the accident an "act of god." The brewery would stand for another century, finally being demolished in 1922. The unusual disaster caused other breweries to slowly phase out the wooden vats in favor of concrete-lined vats. The tragedy is remembered every October at a small pub near the former site of the brewery, where a special vat of porter is brewed to mark the anniversary of the beer flood.

L.A. Dam Break Tragedy

It was built to quench the thirst of a rapidly growing community. Dubbed the St. Francis dam, the huge concrete structure was expected to bring water to the Los Angeles basin for decades to come. But instead, it would provide a tragic outcome for hundreds nestled below it.

The project was the brainchild of William Mulholland, who taught himself engineering and geology in his spare time. He quickly rose through the ranks and became the Superintendent of the Los Angeles City Water Company in 1886, which later became the city's Water Department. He won accolades for his design of the Los Angeles Aqueduct, which uses gravity to bring water from the Owens Valley in central California to Los Angeles. The aqueduct still supplies water to Los Angeles.

While planning the huge project, Mulholland also dreamed of a large reservoir where water could be stored in the event of drought. He found a site in the San Francisquito Canyon, and tested the area for its stability. Once satisfied, construction began, despite concerns he himself had expressed about the region.

Work on the St. Francis Dam began in December of 1922, and finished on May 4, 1926. It was an imposing sight, rising 185 feet above the canyon floor, and holding back a crushing 38,000 acre feet of water. The dam also had a distinctive stair step design.

But problems began almost immediately after its' completion. As water began to fill the reservoir, cracks started to develop, including two large vertical cracks that ran down through the dam from the top. Mulholland inspected the cracks and determined they were within expectation for a concrete dam of that size. Sizable cracks continued to appear over the next few years.

On the morning of March 12, 1928, the dam keeper found a new leak, this one in the west abutment of the dam. Mulholland came out to investigate, and determined the problem needed to be fixed, although the repairs could be done in the near future. The wait would prove tragic.

Just before midnight on March 12, the huge concrete dam failed. The last person to see the dam intact was a carpenter who rode by minutes before the collapse; he heard what sounded like the roar of a motorcycle but assumed it was one of the frequent rockslides in the area.

The dam's failure was complete, and quick. It broke into several large pieces, releasing more than 12 million gallons almost instantaneously. The huge flood wall rushed down the canyon, taking out the cottage of the dam keeper and his family. The 120-foot high wave surged forward at close to 20 miles an hour, destroying a heavy concrete powerhouse and taking the lives of 64 workers and family members who lived nearby.

The rush of water continued downstream, taking out power poles and causing a blackout in Los Angeles. The next target would be the Santa Clarita valley, where a temporary construction camp had been set up by the electric company. No warning was issued, and 84 workers died in the rushing flood waters.

A Santa Clara telephone operator received a frantic message from the chief operator of the Pacific Long Distance Telephone Company, saying the St. Francis Dam had collapsed and a huge wall of water was sweeping downstream. She immediately called Highway Patrol officer Thornton Edwards, who lived nearby, to warn of the danger. Officer Edwards and fellow motorcycle officer Stanley Baker criss-crossed the streets in the danger zone with sirens blaring, to alert residents of the coming danger. The move was a success, with the streets abandoned just prior to the huge wall of water moving through. Many ranches and dairy farms were lost, but the warning saved many lives.

The flood heavily damaged the towns of Bardsdale and Fillmore, and devastated much of Santa Paula, before emptying into the Pacific Ocean. Bodies were recovered as far south as Mexico, and the death toll climbed to an estimated 425 people. It was the largest single loss of life in California, with the exception of the great San Francisco earthquake of 1906.

Los Angeles Dam Tragedy

In the aftermath of the tragedy, the dam site became a grim tourist attraction, with people collecting pieces of the failed structure as souvenirs. The St. Francis Dam was not rebuilt, and a nearby dam was constructed as a replacement.

Mulholland faced a Coroner's inquest, in which he shouldered the blame for the dam's failure, saying "if there was an error in human judgment, I was the human; I won't try to fasten it on anyone else." The inquest determined the cause as an error in engineering judgment assessment, and cleared Mulholland and the Bureau of Water Works of any criminal charges, saying no one could know the instability of the rock formations on which the dam was built.

Mulholland retired about a year later, and retreated to a life of semi-isolation, dying in 1935 at the age of 79.

Today at the site, broken chunks of concrete and rusted handrails can still be seen by visitors, and the site is registered as a California Historic Landmark. A mass grave for victims of the disaster is located at Ivy Lawn Memorial Park in Ventura. Numerous fictional references are made to the St. Francis Dam and the California Water Wars, in the 1974 movie *Chinatown*.

The Great Johnstown Flood Tragedy

It's known simply as the "Great Flood of 1889." But the name does little to reveal the true loss of life and property felt by the residents of Johnstown, Pennsylvania that spring day.

It was May 31, 1889. The town experienced the worst rainstorm in it's history, with Army Engineers estimating six to ten inches of rain in the previous 24 hours. The water swelled Lake Conemauch, held back by the South Fork Dam. The dam was less than 20 years old but known for frequently springing leaks, which were often repaired using mud and straw. Additionally, a previous owner removed the three cast iron discharge pipes which allowed for the controlled release of water, selling the pipes as scrap.

Elias Unger, President of the South Fork Hunting and Fishing club, which owned the dam, awoke to find the water cresting the dam.

He assembled a group of men to help, but a broken fish trap and debris were trapping the rising waters. Others tried plowing the earth to try and raise the top of the dam, with no success. Unger sent John Parker to the South Fork telegraph office to warn the city of Johnstown about the eroding dam. But the warnings were not passed on to authorities, because of previous false alarms.

Johnstown was already prone to flooding because of it's location at the bottom of a steep valley. Residents awoke that fateful morning of May 31 to find their homes slowly being consumed by flood waters as high as ten feet, trapping many in their dwellings. Bad, but worse was to come.

About 3:10 that afternoon, the South Fork Dam collapsed. 20 million tons of water raced down the valley, first slamming into the town of South Fork. Fortunately, the city was on high ground, and many escaped by simply running up hills from the rising water. But that wasn't the case in Johnstown. The flood gathered debris such as houses and fallen trees, briefly being stopped by a railroad bridge. But the sheer force of the water caused the bridge to collapse, and the flood waters resumed their deadly trek.

The village of Mineral Point was the next target. The flood waters slammed into the town, destroying the homes of about 30 people, killing 16. East Conemauch was next. One witness said the flood was like a "huge hill rolling over and over." A train engineer saved many lives when he saw the flood coming, by throwing his engine in reverse, whistle blaring, to warn the people, until the flood reached the engine and tossed it aside like a toy. The engineer survived, but at least 50 people on the train died.

The next target was Woodvale, which lost 314 people in the flood. Then came Johnstown. Residents were caught by surprise by the surge of water and debris, which was traveling at an estimated 40 miles per hour.

The Great Johnstown Flood Tragedy

The flood waters were as high as 60 feet in some places. Victims either drowned or were crushed by pieces of debris. The gigantic wave of water and debris surged over the top of a temporary dam at Johnstown's Stone Bridge, causing the lake water behind the dam to roll upstream. But gravity brought the water back, causing a second wave to hit Johnstown from the opposite direction. Even worse, the debris at the Stone Bridge caught fire; victims who had been washed down into the debris were now trapped by the flames, which killed an estimated 80 people. The fire burned for three days.

As the flood waters finally receded, residents returned to find their homes in ruins. A full-grown tree could be seen sticking out the window of one house. Four square miles of downtown Johnstown were destroyed.

The death toll was staggering. 2,209 people were lost, including 99 entire families, and 396 children. One-third of the dead were never identified, and were buried in the Plot of the Unknown in Grandview Cemetery in Westmont. One of the first responders after the tragedy was nurse Clara Barton, founder of the Red Cross, which stayed on scene for five months. Close to four-million dollars was collected for the Johnstown relief effort, from U.S. citizens and 18 foreign countries.

Critics charged the South Fork Fishing and Hunting Club with not maintaining the dam properly, causing the catastrophe. The club fought the allegations in court, and was never held responsible for the disaster. Instead, the court ruled the tragedy as an act of god.

At Point Park in Johnstown, where the Stonycreek and Little Conemauch rivers meet, an eternal flame burns in memory of the flood victims. Parts of the Stone Bridge have also been made part of a Johnstown Flood Memorial, to remember those lost in the deadly tragedy.

St. Felix Flood Tragedy

It became known as "evil Saturday." A flood so catastrophic it nearly destroyed two whole towns, and ultimately wiped another from the map.

The tragedy began November 5, 1530, on Saint Felix day. A huge storm saturated the town of Zeeland and Oost-Watering in the Netherlands. Eighteen villages were situated in the area. As the floodwaters rose, large parts of Zeeland were washed away. Oost-Watering was flooded, and destroyed. Portions of the nearby city of Reimerswaal were spared because it sat higher than the other towns, but it would be left isolated as a small island. The town of Noord- Beveland was so hard hit, that only its tower of Kortgene was left visible. Attempts to dam the high waters failed.

The death toll was staggering. More than 100,000 people were killed, making it one of the deadliest floods in human history. The few remaining citizens of Reimerswaal soon left, and now nothing remains of the city which had survived for hundreds of years. Some have even called it a medieval "Atlantis." As Netherlands literally translates to "low country," it's not surprising that the region was so devastated by the floodwaters.

About 50-percent of the Netherlands is located about

a meter below sea level. Elaborate drainage systems using dikes, canals, and pumping stations have only proved to be minimally effective at keeping out the potentially deadly waters.

Yellow River Flood Tragedies

A flood on the Yellow River in China is one of the deadliest natural disasters ever recorded in the history of the planet. It was an enormous flood which killed nearly four million people. And it wasn't the first time the Yellow river claimed as many as a million lives.

The tragedy really began in 1928, when for three years a terrible drought affected northern China. Then the storms came. In late 1930, heavy snowstorms were reported, which led to a huge spring thaw. River levels began to rise, and the problem only worsened when heavy spring rains deluged the area. More storms in July and August of 1931 would set the table for disaster, including at least eight cyclones.

With rains recorded as high as 24 inches in just two months, the Yellow River flood began its march across the land. The capital city of China at the time, Nanjing, was swamped by the rising waters. The results were catastrophic. It's believed millions of people died in the resulting floodwaters, and more would succumb to disease such as cholera or typhus. The lack of food led many to starve, and drove some to resort to cannibalism.

The tragedy was far from over. On August 25, water rushed through the Grand Canal near Gaoyou Lake, washing the dikes away as though they didn't exist. An estimated 200,000 people drowned in their sleep, never knowing of the approaching danger. At its peak, the flood waters were an estimated 53 feet above normal.

As shocking as the 1931 loss of life was, it was not the first time the area had been hit with tragedy. While the great flood of 1887 struck in September of that year, its' roots date back hundreds of years earlier. For centuries, farmers living near the Yellow River built and maintained dikes to hold back the water from decimating farmlands.

But over time, silt accumulated in the riverbed, which caused the river to slowly rise unseen.

In September of 1887, a storm dropped heavy rain for several straight days in Northern China. Slowly, the river began to swell. The unrelenting waters began to fill nearby dikes to capacity, finally causing a failure in Huayuankou near the city of Zhengzhou. The low-lying plains in the area allowed the flood waters to quickly escape and reek havoc over a large area. In all, it's believed the flood covered an estimated 50-thousand square miles. Farming settlements and commercial areas were swamped by the huge deluge. Up to two million people found themselves homeless. Amazingly, most of the victims survived the flood waters. But a lack of basic essentials began to claim lives as people starved to death. Disease also overtook the region, and it's believed most of the lives lost were due to the pandemic which ravaged the area.

In the wake of these disasters, the Chinese Government forged the National Flood Relief Commission in 1931, to attempt to gain control over the problem. Even famous aviator Charles Lindbergh was paid to conduct an aerial survey of the flood zone. The NFRC also secured relief for the victims of the 1931 flood, including badly needed food. Ultimately, more than one million workers would rebuild thousands of miles of dikes, to safely hold the rivers back for generations to come.

Tragedy In The Sky

Grand Canyon Plane Crash Tragedy

The Grand Canyon is truly one of the most wondrous places in the country. A mile-deep gorge carved by nature's hand, it contains brilliant hues of red, gold and copper in it's majestic walls. If you happen to be in the right place at the right time, you can also see a reflection of light shining off pieces of metal near the top of one of the canyon walls. Sadly, this is a tragic souvenir from a deadly mid-air collision, which may have been partly caused by the Canyon's beauty.

The date was June 30, 1956, at 10:30 a.m.. Two passenger planes found themselves in the air over the Grand Canyon; flight 2, a TWA Super Constellation, and flight 718, a United Airlines DC-7. The Super Constellation left Los Angeles about an hour and a half earlier, destined for Kansas City. It was about a half hour behind schedule. Sixty-four passengers and six crew members were on board. The DC-7 also flew from Los Angeles, departing just minutes before flight two. It was headed to Chicago's Midway Airport with 53 passengers and five crew members.

Shortly after takeoff, TWA's captain asked for permission to climb to 21,000 feet to avoid a row of thunder heads directly in front of him. The request was denied, but the TWA airliner was allowed to fly 1,000 feet above the thunder heads. Ironically, this put him at 21,000 feet, the same altitude as the DC-7.

As both aircraft approached the Grand Canyon, now at the same altitude, it's believed both planes passed through the same cloud formation, meaning they couldn't see each other. At the last second, the DC-7 banked hard to the right and down, in what investigators believe was a desperate attempt to miss the now-visible Super Constellation. But the maneuver was futile. The DC-7's left wing clipped the top of the TWA's tail vertical stabilizer, and slammed into the fuselage near the tail assembly, causing the tail to break away and fall from the TWA plane. The DC-7's left propeller also struck the TWA fuselage, tearing holes which caused instant decompression, scattering the personal belongings of the victims over a wide area.

Terminally wounded, the TWA plane fell straight down into the Grand Canyon, crashing into the northeast slope of Temple Butte and bursting into flames. The DC- 7, mangled in the crash, fell more slowly but in just as deadly a descent, crashing into the south side cliff of Chuar Butte, where it also caught fire. While no one saw the collision, radio operators in both Salt Lake City and San Francisco heard a garbled transmission saying "Salt Lake, 718, we're going in! Pull up, pull up!" at the time of the crash.

Both planes were reported missing a short time later. The pilots of a small Grand Canyon air taxi service saw the TWA fire, but waived it off as a lighting strike. When they later heard of the crash, the duo took to the skies and circled the site of the fire, where they spotted the fuselage of the Super Constellation. The following day, the two men were also able to find the wreckage of the DC-7.

Grand Canyon Plane Crash Tragedy

Helicopters were brought in to try and recover the victims, but the task was made especially difficult by the rugged terrain. It took years to remove most of the wreckage from the two sites. Sadly, no bodies were recovered intact, and positive identification of the victims was not possible. On July 9, 1956, a mass funeral was held for the United Flight victims, 29 of whom were buried in four coffins at Grand Canyon Pioneer Cemetery. Sixty of the TWA victims were buried in a mass grave at Citizens Cemetery in nearly Flagstaff, Arizona, where a plaque honors their memory.

Investigators determined the two pilots involved in the crash simply didn't see each other until it was too late. However, it's also believed one of the pilots was attempting to provide passengers with a scenic view of the Grand Canyon prior to the crash. While neither flight crew was implicated in the accident, investigators say the decision of TWA's captain to fly 1,000 feet over the clouds put him on a deadly path with the DC-7. The Grand Canyon mid-air collision, killed 128 people making it the deadliest commercial airline disaster in the U.S. up to that point. In April 2014, the site of the crash was declared a National Historic Landmark.

Although the location is closed to the public, at the right time on sunny days in the canyon, you can still see the reflection of aircraft metal laying silently on the canyon walls.

Balloon Bomb Tragedy

Many people assume that the only loss of American lives on American soil during World War Two came in the tragic Pearl Harbor attack. But the war would find victims in Oregon of all places, and those involved proved to be a minister and his wife and students, all in the wrong place at the wrong time.

The culprit was an evil Japanese device known as a "balloon bomb." During the 1940s, Project Fugo was born. The idea was to use the jet stream which sweeps across the Pacific Ocean and into North America. To do this, Japanese scientists designed huge balloons, similar to the atmospheric balloons used today for weather gathering. But these balloons were made of lightweight paper, similar to a Japanese lantern. About 33 feet in diameter and 70 feet tall, they could carry up to 1,000 pounds. Attached to the balloons were high-powered explosives, including a 33-pound fragmentation bomb.

The plan was simple. If the Japanese couldn't directly bomb U.S. targets in North America, it would float the balloon bombs across the Pacific using the jet stream, where they would eventually come down and cause havoc. The trip only took a few days. More than 9,000 of the deadly devices were launched.

People in the U.S. began sighting the balloon bombs

in late 1944, in states like Montana, Wyoming and Nebraska. But each one either exploded before reaching the ground, or crashed harmlessly into the earth.

But some created problems, as the one which touched down into power lines in Washington state, causing a power outage at the Hanford Engineer Works. At the time, Hanford was a key nuclear facility involved in the top secret atomic bomb project. It was where the U.S. was conducting one of it's secret projects to make plutonium for the atom bomb which would ultimately end the war.

Project Fugo was far worse for an Oregon group, where one of the bombs proved deadly.

On May 5, 1945, minister Archie Mitchell took his pregnant wife Elsie and their five students on a picnic near Bly, Oregon. Mitchell parked the car, and Elsie and the children headed to Leonard Creek. Mitchell later remembered: "As I got out of the car to bring the lunch, the others were not far away, and called to me that they had found something that looked like a balloon. I'd heard of Japanese balloons so I shouted a warning not to touch it. But just then there was a big explosion. I ran up there—and they were all dead."

The explosion created a huge three foot wide hole in the ground. Bomb fragments were found 400 feet from the explosion site. The six people who died were Elsie Mitchell, 26; Dick Patzke, 14; Jay Gifford, 13; Edward Engen, 13; Joan Patzke, 13; and Sherman Shoemaker, 11.

A front-page story in the May 7, 1945, *Klamath Falls Herald and News* provided no details, saying only the

six were killed "by an explosion of unannounced cause." Sadly, the victims might have been saved had the government not asked the news media to censor reports about the balloon bombs

Balloon Bomb Tragedy

falling around the U.S. The reporting ban was lifted a week after the tragedy.

A small stone monument was dedicated to the victims on August 20, 1950. Oregon's Governor Douglas McKay said of the victims, "they are casualties of war just as surely as if they had been in uniform."

The balloon bombing deaths remain the only place on the continental United States where Americans were killed by enemy action during World War II.

Fort Dix Tragedies

It was the scene of three unthinkable tragedies in just seven years. Fort Dix army base, located near Trenton, New Jersey, has had its' share of calamities. But three major accidents, just years apart, helped seal its place in history.

The first incident happened in July of 1949. An Eastern Airlines DC-3 passenger plane was in the skies over New Jersey, headed to Memphis, Tennessee. Two other commercial pilots would later complain that a Navy fighter jet was "buzzing" their planes, flying close and then whizzing by. Witnesses suggested the military craft may have been doing the same thing to a small piper cub, when it slammed into the DC-3 in the skies over Fort Dix. The crash sheared off the tail of the passenger plane, which then lost a wing as it twirled toward the ground. It slammed into a farm pasture and burst into flame.

Farmers in the area rushed to the scene to help, but the flames were so intense it kept rescuers away for more than half an hour. All 15 people on board were killed. Most were burned beyond recognition. The pilot of the Navy jet, identified as 26-year-old Robert Poe, was also found dead, his unopened parachute lying nearby.

Just two years later, tragedy would re-visit Fort Dix.

In August of 1951, a T-33 fighter training jet failed shortly after takeoff, while in the skies over the army base. Down below, a group of soldiers were preparing to leave for a communications exercise. Without warning, the jet, on fire and spraying fuel, appeared out of the sky, on a collision course with the soldiers.

Fort Dix Tragedies

Witnesses said it was like watching a ball of fire come out of the sky. Those on the ground dropped and covered their heads, but a group of soldiers inside a transport truck weren't so lucky. They were doused with the flaming fuel and caught in the fireball created by the crashing T-33. Thirteen people were killed, including pilot William Raub, and passenger Theodore Deakyne. 20 more people were injured, though none seriously. Most of the victims had been in the Army less than five months.

The third tragedy was by far the largest. In July of 1956, a C-118 military transport plane lifted off from the base in stormy weather, headed for Burtonwood, England. On board were 56 passengers, including six civilians, two of which were children. A flight crew of ten manned the aircraft. Just a short time after the plane took off, radio contact was lost. Witnesses on board the doomed craft said later that the airline hit an air pocket and split in two, spreading debris along a half-mile area.

It crashed in a swampy pine forest, and amazingly, did not burn, allowing for some to escape. It took rescuers several hours to find the crash site in a lightning storm, which turned the scene into a quagmire. Victims had to be carried from the plane by hand. This crash killed 45 people, including the two children, and 21 others were injured.

It was a startling number of tragedies for one area; three in seven years, all military related.

Personal Tragedies

Child in Well Tragedy

Many may still remember the drama surrounding the rescue of baby Jessica from an abandoned well in Midland, Texas, back in 1987. But another attempted rescue of a child who fell down a well captivated the whole country in 1949, and was one of the first tragedies ever captured on live television.

The drama began on a sunny day in San Marino, California, on Friday, April 8. Three-year old Kathy Fiscus was playing with her nine-year-old sister Barbara, and a cousin, Gus. Then, Gus heard a scream. He investigated and found that little Kathy had fallen through the 14-inch opening of an old water well, and dropped to the bottom, 100 feet down. Ironically, Kathy's father David worked for the California Water and Telephone Company, and had recently testified before the state legislature that the old water well openings around Los Angeles should be cemented over for safety.

The children ran for help. Soon, dozens of would-be rescuers were at the site. The little trapped girl could be heard speaking and crying, which gave hope to those on the scene.

A short time later, a major rescue operation was underway. Drills, derricks, three giant cranes, bulldozers and trucks from several nearby towns were brought in to help. Hollywood even lent a hand by supplying 50 studio floodlights to help rescuers see. But the process was slow, and soon the little girl's cries could not be heard. Rescuers intensified their efforts, digging through Friday night into Saturday, and continuing through Sunday Morning. Down 100 feet to finally reach the child on Sunday night. A doctor was quickly lowered down the rescue hole, and reached the girl. He used a public address system to make the announcement to the crowd. Tragically, she was already dead, having suffocated. The only solace, according to the doctor, was that the little girl had probably died a short time after falling into the well, and didn't suffer long. Tired, dirty, and beaten, rescuers who had been digging for 40 hours openly wept.

The tragedy brought people all over the country together. It was carried by live television with KTLA reporter Stan Chambers narrating the event, beginning on Saturday. Live radio was also on the scene. Viewers and listeners were glued to their TV sets and radios, hoping the little girl would be found alive. Neighbors who had barely spoken to each other now sat together, transfixed by the coverage. The 27- hour live broadcast of the rescue attempt was considered a groundbreaking turning point in television history, despite the tragic ending.

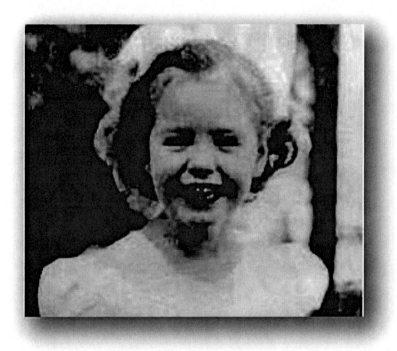

Child in Well Tragedy

On a hillside at the upper field of San Marino High School sits an abandoned well, unmarked except for a cement cover. The body of little Kathy Fiscus was taken for burial at Glen Abbey Memorial Park in Bonita, California. Her inscription reads "One little girl who united the world for a moment." Country singer Jimmie Osborne wrote and sang the 1949 ballad "The Death of Little Kathy Fiscus" which sold over a million copies.

The singer donated half the earnings to the Fiscus family.

Hotel Walkway Collapse

It was the deadliest structure collapse in U.S. history, surpassed only by 9/11. What began as a celebration ended as a tragic reminder of poor design and construction, which left dozens dead.

The tragedy began the night of July 17, 1981. About 1,600 people were gathered in the atrium of the Hyatt Regency Hotel in Kansas City, Missouri, to watch a tea dance.

Many stood on two connected walkways that hovered over the floor several stories up. One bridge, four stories up, was suspended directly over the second story bridge. A third floor walkway was just yards away.

The fun was in full swing when without warning, the fourth story bridge filled with people failed. It crashed down onto the second story bridge, also filled with people, and both came crashing to the ground. The atrium was choked with dust and debris, and the sounds of moaning victims.

Emergency personnel rushed to the scene, to begin the grim task of digging out possible survivors. But the job proved too great for firefighters; those trapped were buried under more than 60 tons of steel, concrete and glass, and the fire department's most powerful jacks could not lift the debris. The call went out to construction companies in the area, along with building supply stores. They assembled an army of hydraulic jacks, acetylene torches, compressors and generators. Cranes were brought in to lift sections of the fallen walkways. A makeshift morgue was established in a ground floor exhibition area, with the hotel's driveway and front lawn used as a triage area.

Hotel Walkway Collapse

The recovery was grim. Some were injured so badly they would not survive; instead, they were given morphine to ease the pain. In some cases, rescuers had to dismember dead bodies to reach survivors. One victim even had to have his leg removed with a chain saw, because it had been crushed by a falling steal beam. His life was saved.

Some of the victims almost drowned while waiting for rescue. The building's fire sprinkler system was damaged, and water flooded the atrium. Finally, a fire chief realized the danger, and had a bulldozer smash open the hotel's front doors, which were acting as a dam to keep the rising waters in. In all, 114 were killed, and 216 injured in the catastrophe.

Three days after the disaster, an investigation discovered a change to the original construction plan made the design only about 60-percent capable of handling the minimum load required by building codes.

The new design had the fourth floor beams being required to support both the fourth and second floors. The engineers for the company which approved the final plans were found culpable of gross negligence, misconduct, and unprofessional conduct in the practice of engineering. All lost their licenses. At least $140 million dollars was awarded to victims and their families.

The hotel has since been renamed the Sheraton Kansas City at Crown Center. A memorial to the victims was dedicated on November 12, 2015, more than 34 years after the tragedy.

Reporter Live Suicide

It was her dream to someday be a television reporter.

And with some hard work and a little luck, Christine Chubbuck achieved her dream. But the 29-year-old faced a number of demons which led to her dramatic and tragic exit from the airways.

Chubbuck earned a degree in broadcasting from Boston University in 1965. She went to work for WVIZ in Cleveland for a year, but briefly got out of the business to work as a hospital computer operator. Chubbuck got back into television with a front office job at WTOG in St. Petersburg, Florida, before landing the reporter job at WXLT in Sarasota.

She was given a community affairs talk show called *Suncoast Digest,* which featured local people and activities. Chubbuck took the position seriously, engaging local political figures on the matters of interest to the growing beach community. She was even nominated for a Forestry and Conservation Recognition Award for her service on the talk show.

But Chubbuck kept a deep secret hidden from everyone. She struggled her whole life with depression and suicidal thoughts.

She once attempted to kill herself with an overdose, and was seeing a psychiatrist until several weeks prior to her death. She also told co-workers she was depressed because she was almost 30 and still a virgin, who had never been on more than two dates with a man. In addition, Chubbuck also had an ovary removed, and her doctor said if she didn't get pregnant within the next three years, it was unlikely she would ever get pregnant. To make matters worse, she had a crush on a fellow newsperson at the station, George Peter Ryan, even going so far as to bake him a cake. He, however, was interested in another employee at the station, which could only have fueled Chubbuck's depression.

In the weeks before her death, Chubbuck did a story on suicides, talking with the police about the best methods. A week before her suicide, she told the nightly news editor she'd bought a gun, and joked about killing herself on the air. He didn't take it seriously, calling it a sick joke.

On the morning of July 15th, 1974, Chubbuck confused her director by asking that the live show be recorded on tape, and that she planned to open the talk show by reading several news reports.

Once on air, Chubbuck read four stories, then looked into the camera and said, "In keeping with Channel 40's policy of bringing you the latest in 'blood and guts', and in living color, you are going to see another first, a live broadcast of an attempted suicide."

Before the startled director could react, she jerked out her .38 caliber pistol and shot herself behind the right ear.

Reporter Live Suicide

Chubbuck fell forward violently onto the desk, and the director faded the broadcast rapidly to black. The station quickly switched to a movie. Callers began inquiring, wondering if the shooting was staged.

Chubbuck died 14 hours later at a local hospital. The script from which she was reading contained the wording not only of the shooting, but an account to be read on-air later, to the effect of, "TV 40 news personality Christine Chubbuck shot herself in a live broadcast this morning." She also left a suicide note for her family, in which she said she wanted to take her life in this way, to emphasize her opinion of blood and guts news reporting. Her body was cremated; the ashes scattered in the Gulf of Mexico.

For decades it was thought the grizzly footage had been lost. But in June of 2016 the widow of station owner Robert Nelson confirmed she had a copy, which she had given to a lawyer for safekeeping.

She has no plans to release the footage to the public. Without the easy cell phone video available today, it is unlikely the grisly event will ever be seen again.

America's Worst Mining Disaster

Coal mining was a staple of American life in the late nineteenth and early twentieth century. But it was a dangerous occupation, which often led to the deaths of workers. The worst of these disasters came on December 6, 1907, in the small town of Monongah, West Virginia, and is remembered not only for the tragic loss of life, but the heroic rescue efforts put forth by many volunteers.

The Monongah mines were located about six miles south of Fairmont, on the west fork of the Monongahela river. They were considered to be cutting-edge mines in terms of technology and safety, with electricity being used for the coal-cutting machinery, and large fans in place for ventilation. Instead of back-breaking labor, locomotives were used to haul the coal up from inside the mines.

It was a routine day in the early morning hours when something went horribly wrong. At 10:28 a.m. a sudden and massive explosion ripped through the number 6 and number 8 mines at the facility. The blast shook the earth up to eight miles away. Nearby buildings were shattered, and both people and horses were knocked to the ground by the fierce blast. Streetcars were even knocked off their rails.

Smoke billowed from deep inside the mines as rescuers rushed to the scene. They were met with a frustrating picture. Every local mine official was missing, and chaos reigned at the entrances of the mines. Shortly after the explosion, four bleeding miners emerged from the smoke, dazed and confused but essentially unharmed. But hundreds of miners remained down below, and the survivors had no news of their fellow workers.

Hundreds came from the town to the site of the disaster; along with volunteers were hundreds of shrieking women and children whose loved ones were still trapped down below. The volunteers began to clear the debris at the mine entrance, but were forced back by the toxic air spewing from inside. Some even had to be rescued themselves. The blast had wrecked one of the large ventilation fans in the Number 8 mine, making the conditions even worse.

As the volunteers slowly made their way into the mine, what they found was a disastrous scene. Choking coal dust gave way to rubble and wrecked equipment.

Coal cars were smashed and piled one on top of the other. Air shafts had been blown out, the bricks which made them scattered about. Rescuers were forced to use canvas curtains as they slowly made their way into the mines, the partitions helping to block the dust and soot, and restore ventilation.

Six hours into the rescue mission, a low moaning sound was heard near a crop hole. A rescuer was lowered into the hole by rope, and discovered miner Peter Urban sitting on the dead body of his brother, Stanislaus. Peter sobbed uncontrollably as he was rescued. He would be the last survivor of the Monongah tragedy.

America's Worst Mining Disaster

The searchers never gave up hope, although as the days wore on the scope of the disaster became very apparent. Bodies had to be hauled as far as 3,000 feet through a minefield of fallen roof timbers, wrecked ore cars, broken machinery and electrical wiring. The exhausted volunteers faced intense heat and poor ventilation, many coming up out of the mines with headaches and nausea. Sadly, they also had to deal with the stench of death, with became stronger each passing day.

Along with the volunteers, embalmers found themselves working around the clock. Caskets bearing the dead lined the main street. The bank even served as a makeshift morgue. Church services were held several times a day as more victims were discovered and brought to the surface. The remains were often difficult to identify, and some bodies were claimed by more than one family.

It took nearly a full week to recover the remaining bodies entombed inside the mine. The death toll was staggering. 337 bodies were found amid the ruins, with another 25 victims found later during cleanup operations.

However, some experts have estimated the death toll at more like 500. The 362 official casualties of the Monongah mine disaster left more than a thousand widows and children behind.

An investigation by the Marion County Coroner's Jury concluded the victims died from an explosion, possibly caused by an electrical spark, or an open flame from a miner's lantern which ignited blasting powder in mine number eight.

The disaster was one of several which caused Congress in 1910 to create a special U.S. Bureau of Mines, with the goal of both limiting tragedies like the Monongah mine, and creating better working conditions with less waste of natural resources.

For the victims, a special graveyard was laid out on a nearby hillside, where hundreds were buried in the half- frozen ground. A granite marker at the Mount Calvary Cemetery honors those who died in the tragic blast.

Church Stampede Tragedy

When one thinks of a deadly stampede, one tends to turn to visions of horses or elephants scrambling out of control. But sadly, humans can also be the bearers of deadly stampedes, as thousands discovered in Alabama in 1902.

The date was September 19. The place, the Shiloh Baptist Church in Birmingham. It was, at the time, the largest black church in the city. On that day, about 3,000 people came to hear famous speaker and founder of the Tuskegee Institute, Booker T. Washington, address the National Convention of Negro Baptists.

The tragedy began innocently enough. A convention delegate reportedly began to quarrel with the local choir leader over a seat. The argument escalated, and one man appeared to pull a gun. Someone in the choir yelled "fight!" The nearby crowd, thinking they had heard the word "fire," got up en masse and began to exit the building. Seeing what was happening, a minister came to the podium and yelled for "quiet." But an even larger number of people, convinced they heard the word "fire", began a rush to safety. People began screaming as men and women crawled over the pews to try and escape, trampling those who had fallen.

The design of the church also proved to be a

deathtrap. The steps leading up to the entryway were fifteen feet off the ground. Those first few who reached the tops of the steps were pushed violently from behind and fell all the way to the ground; others fell on top of them, until a human pile about five feet high developed. At least twenty people at the bottom died of suffocation.

Church Stampede Tragedy

Two men at the rear of the church realized the seriousness of the situation, and quickly called for the fire department. Fire wagons arrived to scatter the crowd outside the church, and police officers came soon after.

The scene was chaotic. Scores of people lost their footing on the high steps and fell to the bottom, suffering broken bones. Rescuers went inside the church to find dozens of people trampled to death in the aisles; others cried out for help, too wounded to move. The victims were laid out in the street; that is where many stayed until the early hours of the morning, before they could be moved.

The death toll was staggering. 115 people were pronounced dead from the stampede. Many of the victims were women, and most were from Birmingham. Because they suffocated from being trampled, the scene was a bizarre sight of victims appearing to be asleep, as there was no blood or sign of injury. Speaker Booker T. Washington escaped without injury; but, the tragedy reportedly haunted him until the end of his life.

Carolean Death March Tragedy

Many are familiar with the story of the Bataan Death March of World War Two, when Japanese troops forced American and Filipino troops to undergo a grueling and deadly prisoner march in April of 1942, killing as many as 20,000. But it would not be the first time in history that a death march would take thousands of lives; and on one occasion, the march was instigated by the troops themselves.

The year was 1719. The Swedish army had recently lost eastern territories to Russia in the Great Northern War. It had also suffered losses in Norway. About six-thousand exhausted and starved soldiers were in retreat; their only thought was to get home alive. Bad weather kept the troops from getting much-needed supplies from Sweden, and the army had to live off the land.

On January 7, Lieutenant-general Carl Gustaf Armfeldt received word that Charles XII of Sweden had died. The general was ordered back to Sweden, and chose to take what he thought would be the shortest route back: over the mountains to Tydal, and then over the Tydal mountains to the fort of Hjerpe. The first movement of the long march would be to Tydal, about 30 miles away.

The cold weather began to set in, and about 200 soldiers would die of exposure on the trip. But the worst was yet to come.

The surviving soldiers left Tydal on January 12. The march was expected to take two days. But mother nature had other plans. That afternoon a violent blizzard struck, blinding the troops with snow and leaving them in biting cold. On the first night, soldiers began to burn their rifle butts and sleds to try and keep warm, but the brutal conditions caused about 200 men to freeze to death that first night.

The storm continued the next day. Cold, tired, and hungry, the troops began to become separated in the conditions, as they tried to continue marching toward safety. The main force reached the Swedish border and camped on the Ena river; they even chopped through the ice to see which way the water was flowing, because they knew that was the direction home. But the storm was unyielding, and many of the horses died. All of the equipment would soon be left abandoned.

The heartiest of the survivors continued their march to Handol, arriving on the January 15 and 16. But the trek took a deadly toll. About 3,000 men remained on the mountain, frozen to death. And the nightmare wasn't over. As the remaining troops marched to the town of Duved, another 700 would die on that trip. All told, about 5,800 men would perish on the death march.

The aftermath was brutal. As the weather cleared,

rescuers went up into the mountains to find hundreds of dead soldiers. One was found attempting to drive a frozen cart, his final glazed expression showing where he met his end. Local residents would soon plunder the coats, boots, and valuables of the dead. Even the wild animals of the area would capitalize by feeding on hundreds of frozen remains.

In the town of Duved stands a memorial to the soldiers who died in the Carolean Death March. A outdoor theater production is also held every year to dramatize the tragic events. While in Roros, an annual open-air musical is staged every other year, and draws large crowds of those wishing to understand the tragedy.

Mt. Pelee Volcano Tragedy

A volcanic eruption is a dangerous and often deadly event. Such was the case for the village of St. Pierre on the French Caribbean island of Martinique. But it wasn't just lava flows which caused people and animals to be killed; it was something else which crawled out of the volcanic ground, something geologists call a Fiery Cloud eruption.

It was January 1902 when Mount Pelee began to show signs of life. The smoking volcano offered little concern to the public for months, until April 23, when minor explosions were heard at the summit of the volcano. The blasts shook residents of St. Pierre over the next few days. Then the town was showered in ash from the volcano, and enveloped in a thick cloud of choking gas. But the nightmare was only beginning.

The city and the outer areas were suddenly besieged by an invasion of snakes and poisonous insects. Horses, pigs and dogs screamed as red ants and foot-long centipedes crawled up their legs and bit them. Thousands of poisonous snakes were also awakened by the volcano, and slithered into town, biting humans and animals alike. It was a scene straight out of a horror movie. About 200 animals died of snake bites. For the humans, it was a time of terror, as families tried to drive the snakes out of their homes with little luck. The poisonous reptiles targeted everything in their path. It's estimated about 50 people were killed by the venomous snake bites, most of them children.

Mt. Pelee Volcano Tragedy

As terrifying as the situation was, it would grow even worse. At 7:50 a.m. on May 8, the volcano erupted with a deafening roar. A large black cloud of superheated gas, ash and rock raced down the mountainside at a speed of 100 miles an hour, headed straight for St. Pierre. It struck with the force of a hurricane. Meter-thick masonry walls were blown into rubble. Support girders were twisted like pretzels. The searing heat ignited huge fires. Thousands of barrels of rum stored in warehouses exploded, sending rivers of flaming liquid through the streets.

The advancing cloud even proved to be deadly to those at sea. The blast capsized the steamship *Grappler,* and set fire to the American sailing ship *Roraima,* killing most of the passengers and crew. Those on board could only watch in horror as the cloud descended upon them.

When it was over, and the pyroclastic flow had made it's way to the sea, it left behind a city in ruins. Of the 28,000 people in St. Pierre, only two survived the terrifying wrath of the volcano. Most died within seconds of breathing in the scorching fumes.

In October, five months after the devastating eruption, a lava dome began to rise from the crater floor. It grew for a solid year into the form of an obelisk, soaring 1000 feet over the base of the crater floor. It was dubbed "the tower of Pelee" and stood for about eleven months, before the sheer weight caused it to collapse. The mountain is now considered a non-active volcano, although it registers seismic activity. A sign that it may someday come back to life and once again haunt the citizens of St. Pierre.

Killer Tiger Tragedy

While many tragedies are the result of Mother Nature, some tragedies sprang from the animal kingdom. One such tragedy was so terrible, it's even listed in the Guinness Book of World Records for the unbelievable amount of carnage caused by one large Bengal tiger.

While tiger attacks around the world are nothing new, one particular tiger began to claim victims at an alarming rate in a region of Nepal near the Himalayas, in the late nineteenth century. A huge Bengal tiger was reportedly ambushing villagers by the dozen, as they walked through the jungle. Soon, as the death toll grew to more than 200, hunters were sent in to find and kill the big cat. But the tiger was shrewd, and evaded capture.

Finally, the Nepalese Army was called in to try and find the beast. The move would prove unsuccessful, although the tiger was driven from the area into the Kumaon District of India.

It didn't take long for the killer tiger to begin hunting again. She began to stalk her humans with increasing bravado, killing villagers in broad daylight, and even prowling the town's streets looking for anyone unfortunate enough to be out at the time. People were paralyzed with fear, refusing to leave their huts whenever they heard the tiger roar in the distance. The town was described as a virtual "ghost town" because no one dared be seen outside.

The death toll continued to climb into the four hundreds. It seemed it would take a miracle to end the bloodshed. Finally, in 1907, in the town of Champawat, a 16-year-old girl was ambushed as she gathered firewood, and torn to pieces, leaving a trail of blood and limbs. A British hunter named Jim Corbett decided to follow the grisly trail, and the next day came face to face with the killer beast. Corbett fired his rifle, and the deadly tiger was brought down in front of hundreds of spectators. In all, it's believed the beast killed an astonishing 436 people.

So what caused the tiger to target its rage against humans? An autopsy found the animal had broken the upper and lower canine teeth on the right side of its mouth. Corbett deduced the injury prevented the tiger from hunting her natural prey. Corbett would later kill a male leopard which was terrorizing another district in India; a feline responsible for close to 400 deaths.

In Champawat, near the Chataar Bridge, there is a memorial to the incident; a small cement board marking the place where the deadly tiger was finally brought down after it's terrifying reign.

Elephant Stampede Tragedy

Elephants are often thought of as gentle giants; playful and smart, and eager to entertain. But these behemoths can quickly turn from benign beasts to colossal terrors, leaving a trail of death in their wake. Such was the case in India in 1972.

The date was July 10. The Chandka Forest region was in the grip of a searing heat wave. The area was already dry from a long-running drought, and both humans and animals in the area were feeling the pinch. It was especially noticeable in the local elephant herd.

Normally quite docile, the high heat and lack of food and water appeared to agitate the giants; so much so that local farmers were afraid to tend to their lands, because of the potential elephant danger.

Then, without warning, the elephants exploded. They went berserk and rushed through a village, trampling everything in their paths. Another village was trampled, then another; in all five villages would be demolished by the rampaging herd. The death toll was high. 24 people who were unable to get out of the way found themselves trampled to death by the huge beasts.

Ironically, the area is now very lush and wet, and is actually used as an elephant sanctuary. A far cry from that tragic day in 1972.

Avalanche Tragedies

Tyrolean Avalanche Tragedy

While the weapons of war can be ingenious as well as destructive, sometimes the deadliest encounters occur because of fate. During World War One, several such battles were impacted by the power of mother nature. The deadly power of the avalanche.

The time was 1916. Austrian soldiers had set up barracks near Italy's Mount Marmolada at the base of the Tyrolean Alps. Thousands of soldiers camped there, awaiting their next orders. Above them, heavy snowfall collected on the mountain; as much as 40 feet high in some areas. One Austrian officer reportedly said, "the mountains in winter are more dangerous than the Italians." The conditions were ripe for avalanches.

On December 13, Italian troops advanced, and a battle ensued. Whether it was war that caused the tragedy, or if it was purposely brought to bear by Italian troops, we may never know. But without warning, the side of the mountain began to rain down 200,000 tons of snow, rock and ice, as both sides fought. Fighting stopped as the brunt of the avalanche swept through the battlefield, slamming into the Austrian base camp. The soldiers were helpless to stop the onslaught of snow and ice. When it was over, about 300 troops were buried alive. Another 200 were pulled to safety.

Tyrolean Avalanche Tragedy

But the mountain was far from being quieted. Over the next week, heavy snow and high winds continued to create dangerous conditions, and more avalanches continued to fall on a deadly track through the soldiers. Entire regiments were lost in the blink of an eye. The destruction continued throughout the month. It's estimated as many as 10,000 soldiers died from the series of avalanches that struck the area by the end of December. Some of the bodies would not be discovered until the spring thaw. Amazingly, some remains of soldiers were recovered as many as 80 years later. The ensuing front became known as "the war in ice and snow." Some have suggested the avalanches were planned, but most experts believe the timing was random, although it's possible the detonation of explosives to dig defense tunnels deep in the mountainside may have played a role.

Despite the conditions, fighting continued on the frozen battlefields near the Isonzo river, until 1918. At wars' end, the cold and hungry troops left the mountains for their homes, leaving much of the equipment, and their memories, behind.

Dyatlov Pass Tragedy

It is a tragedy steeped in mystery. The unusual deaths of nine ski hikers in the northern Ural Mountains of Russia, all of whom were considered expert outdoorsmen. What caused the tragedy may forever remain a mystery.

The date was February 2 1959. The group of hikers from the Ural Polytechnical Institute established camp on the slopes of Kholat Syakhl for the night. The area would later be dubbed Dyatlov Pass, in honor of the group's leader, Igor Dyatlov. The hikers were made up of eight men and two women. Their goal was to reach Otorten mountain for skiing. Dyatlov said he would send a telegram to the group's sports club as soon as they returned. But no word came.

It took more than two weeks, but after relatives pleaded for information on the missing hikers, a rescue operation was put into place on February 20. It took six days and the use of military planes and helicopters, but finally, a clue. The groups' badly damaged tent was found on Kholat Syakhl. What remained was a bizarre testimony to what happened. The tent was torn and covered with snow, and investigators believed it had been cut open from the inside. A number of footprints were found leading away from the area, left by people wearing only one shoe, socks, or barefoot. All of the group's belongings were left behind. The tracks wound down about a mile from the campsite, where they were then covered in snow. Searchers found the remains of a small fire, along with two victims, shoeless and dressed only in their underwear. Three other frozen victims were found in poses suggesting they were trying to get back to the original campsite.

It would take another two months to find the four remaining missing travelers. On May 4, their bodies were discovered under about 15 feet of snow. It appeared those who died first gave their clothes to the survivors, with one man wearing a faux fir coat and hat of a female victim.

Of the first five bodies, experts determined hypothermia was the cause of death, although one man had suffered a skull fracture. But the bodies found in May revealed a different story. One had major skull fractures, and two had major chest fractures. One doctor said the force required to make those injuries was the equivalent to being hit by a car. One woman was found missing her tongue, eyes, and part of her lips, although she was found lying face down in a small stream, which probably contributed to her injuries.

So what went wrong? Investigators originally wondered if the group was attacked by the Mansi people, an indigenous group who lived in the area. But there were no signs of a struggle at the campsite. Then there was the radiation. Forensic radiation tests reportedly showed high doses of radioactive material on the clothing of several victims. Investigators would later decide that all of the victims had been killed by a compelling natural force. But decades later, a former police officer who investigated the tragedy would say his team had no rational explanation for the incident, and that after his team reported seeing flying spheres in the area, they received direct orders from high-ranking officials to dismiss the claim.

Dyatlov Pass Tragedy

Other investigators suggest the group awoke in a panic, thinking an avalanche was imminent. They ran to the relative safety of the nearby woods, where the trees would help break up the snow slide. Because it was night, the hikers got separated, and were unable to return to their camp before freezing to death. The most severely injured were probably caught in a deadly avalanche. But other investigator say there were no obvious signs of avalanche in the area, and no expeditions to the region since have reported avalanche conditions. Indeed, a study of the area found the terrain was unlikely to produce an avalanche.

Another theory is that the tragedy was the result of a military accident that was later covered up. Records show parachute mines were being tested at the time by the Russian military; these weapons would have exploded just above ground and created injuries similar to what the hikers suffered, heavy internal damage with little external trauma. The glowing orbs reported in the sky could have been those type of munitions. And one investigation concluded the group was the victim of a vicious Yeti, or Abominable Snow Monster. Say what you will ....

The tragedy led to the founding of the Dyatlov Foundation, to try get Russian officials to re-investigate the mysterious tragedy. There is also a Dyatlov Museum which preserves the memory of the dead hikers. A monument also stands at the Mikhajlov Cemetery in Yekaterinburg, where the victims were buried.

Yungay Avalanche Tragedy

It's known as the deadliest avalanche in recorded history. And unlike many avalanches, which can be set off by noise or heavy accumulation of snow, this one was spawned by a powerful earthquake.

The date was May 31, 1970, in Peru. Residents of the major Peruvian fishing port of Chimbite were going about their daily routine. Before anyone could realize what was happening, a huge earthquake, measured at 7.9, struck offshore, shaking for about 45 seconds. The powerful tremor shook the adobe buildings down to the foundations, collapsing many in the coastal town. It's believed about two-thousand people died in the destruction of the earthquake. But the worst was yet to come.

A glacier high up the mountain of Huascaran was destabilized by the quake. The temblor touched off a gigantic slide of ice and rock, at speeds of 120 miles per hour. The fast-moving mass scooped up massive amounts of glacial deposits and debris estimated at millions of pounds. The landslides' target was the town of Yungay. It only took about three minutes before the village was pummeled by boulders, rock, and snow from above. Many of the 25,000 residents were watching a World Cup soccer match when the quake hit, and many retreated to nearby churches to pray, where they would be crushed by the debris. Some survivors said they heard a low rumble shortly after the quake, then saw a giant cloud of dust and debris racing down the mountain. A giant wave of grey mud slid through the city, and the sky went dark because of the dust. Ironically, about 300 people survived the tragedy by rushing to the cemetery, where they were protected by the higher ground. Another group of survivors were children who had been attending a circus outside of town; a clown reportedly led the children to safety. After Yungay was destroyed, another small village, Ranrahirca, was also buried in the avalanche.

In all, an estimated 80,000 lost their lives, in the worst avalanche in history. At least a million people were left homeless.

The Peruvian government chose to preserve the area as a national cemetery. A new city of Yungay was built just a few miles away.

Two American scientists, David Bernays and Charles Sawyer predicted the disaster. They reported seeing a massive slab of rock being undermined by a glacier, which threatened to slide right down onto the city of Yungay. The Peruvian government ordered the men to retract their findings, or face imprisonment. Instead, they fled the country, and no one spoke of the impending disaster until eight years later, when the prediction came true.

Yungay Avalanche Tragedy

Stormy Tragedies

Hurricane Camille Tragedy

2017 proved to be a disastrous year for the United States in terms of weather, with devastating flooding in Texas and Florida caused by two separate and powerful storms. But it wasn't too long ago that one of the most destructive hurricanes in recorded history slammed into the southern underbelly of the U.S., with terrible consequences.

The storm was dubbed "Camille." It began as a small tropical depression near Cuba on August 14th, 1969. Before it was through, it would grow into the second-largest hurricane to ever strike America.

Camille grew quickly in the warm waters off Cuba, intensifying into a Category 2 Hurricane in just one day. The storm rolled over the western part of the island, on it's trek into the Gulf of Mexico. There, it's fury grew exponentially. By August 16th, just two days after appearing as a tropical depression, Camille was a powerful Category 5 Hurricane, with a pressure reading of 905 mbar, the lowest ever recorded by a reconnaissance aircraft, and the second-lowest ever recorded in the U.S.

The deadly hurricane left Cuba and set its' sights on the southern state of Mississippi. Landfall was made on August 18, in the city of Waveland. Wind speeds of 175 were recorded, but the winds were so strong they knocked out the wind gauges of nearby weather stations, and some have suggested the winds reached 200 miles per hour. Fortunately, many residents heeded the warning of the approaching superstorm, and retreated inland. Camille moved rapidly, dropping only moderate rainfall because of it's speed, but still bringing catastrophic flooding to Alabama, Mississippi, and Louisiana. One-hundred and forty-three deaths are linked to the landfall of the storm. Many of the dead were coastal residents who had ridden out hurricanes before and refused to evacuate. They had never seen anything approaching the power of Camille.

As Camille roared inland, the slowly diminished in size and speed, but still contained vast amounts of moisture. Stalling over the Blue Ridge mountains of Virginia, the storm brought huge mudflows and land slides to the steep mountain slopes along with deadly flooding, with an additional 153 people succumbing to the intense rain, mud, and floods.

The total destruction was devastating. About 8,900 people were injured, with more than 5,600 homes destroyed, and close to 14,000 homes suffering major damage. Total cost was 1.42 billion dollars, making Camille the second-most expensive hurricane in U.S. history up to that time, behind only Hurricane Betsy, which had destroyed parts of Louisiana only four years prior.

One unusual story which grew out of the storm was the tale of the "Hurricane Party." The tale states 23 people gathered on the third floor of the Richelieu Manor Apartments in Christian, Mississippi, to wait out the storm. The eye of the hurricane targeted the area, causing a high surge which knocked the building to the ground. In reality, while 23 people were known to have stayed at the Richelieu during the storm, only eight are confirmed casualties. One survivor, Ben Duckworth, even expressed irritation over the story, saying the people there were too tired from boarding up windows to have thrown any kind of party.

Richelieu Manor Apartments Before (top) and After
Camille (bottom)
Ironically, the site of the apartment complex later became
a shopping center, which was destroyed by Hurricane

Katrina, one of the best known of the more recent hurricanes. The name Camille was retired after the 1969 storm because of the destruction it caused, and will never be used again.

Okeechobee Hurricane Tragedy

It's death toll was second only to the great Galveston hurricane. The Okeechobee Hurricane battered Florida on September 17, 1928 with destructive and deadly force. But the severe winds which blasted the landscape would give way to even deadlier flood waters, which targeted one particular area with frightening precision.

It began as a small storm of the coast of West Africa on September 6. Not content to be confined, the storm commenced a methodical march across the Atlantic, with the first target being Guadeloupe. The now-category 4 hurricane slammed the small Caribbean nation with intense winds, bringing devastation to the small islands. The death toll was staggering at an estimated 1,200 deaths. But the Okeechobee Hurricane was far from done.

The storm increased in intensity to a Category 5 hurricane, with winds at 160 miles per hour. It then set its sights on Puerto Rico, becoming the only category 5 hurricane to ever hit the island. The Weather Bureau sent out warnings every two hours to the citizens, the first hurricane warning ever broadcast by radio. It worked because the death toll of 312 was low compared to Guadeloupe, but the damage was just as severe. About 25,000 homes were destroyed, and another

192,000 were damaged. Several small towns were simply swept away. The carnage left half a million people homeless. The storm's heavy rainfall also destroyed many agricultural areas, doing extensive damage to the vegetation. The total cost here was estimated at 50 million dollars.

The next target would be the Bahamas, although intense preparations for the storm would lead to only 18 lives being lost.

The morning of September 17 found the killer hurricane making landfall near West Palm Beach, Florida. It hit with furious 125 mile an hour winds, which one witness said sounded like a New York City subway train going by at full speed. It brought a storm surge which caused Lake Okeechobee to fill to the brim with water, ultimately destroying the dikes which held the water back from nearby farmlands. People and homes were swept away in the flooding, and close to 2,000 people died

Victims remember people walking the streets with dead babies, asking "Are these your children?" One family said the winds were so strong as to knock their house off it's foundation, breaking it like a cheap toy. Another family tried to escape the flood waters by cutting a hole in the roof of their house, pushing the family piano underneath, and climbing up to what they hoped would be safety.

WEST PALM BEACH SCENES
NORTH END MURAL, N. POINSETTIA   LYTAL PRATT FURNITURE
RIVIERA   CHURCH OF CHRIST ROSEMARY
THIRD ST, ACROSS FROM BARCOB   AND HIBISCUS

Okeechobee Hurricane Tragedy

They were wrong. The house was knocked from it's foundation and was caught up in the raging flood waters. As it twisted and turned, family members fought for their lives, with the home eventually turning upside down in the torrent. Amazingly, a little girl and her stepfather survived; 17 other members of the family did not. At least 2,500 people died in the state of Florida that day, making the storm the second deadliest in the U.S., behind only the great Galveston Hurricane of 1900. It caused at least $25 million dollars in damage in the sunshine state.

Racial segregation of the time period impacted what happened to the bodies in Florida. White victims were buried in coffins, with many being taken to Woodlawn Cemetery in West Palm Beach. Black victims were burned in funeral pyres or dumped into mass graves, including the pauper's cemetery. The Mayor of West Palm Beach called for a day of mourning, and had a memorial placed at Woodlawn Cemetery to honor the victims, where it stands today; no memorial was placed at the pauper's gravesite.

Crete Tsunami Tragedy

The memory of the great killer tsunami of 2004 is still quite vibrant for many. The videos taken by survivors showed the horrifying rush of ocean waters to the world.

It was a truly destructive force, and one that history has recorded on several other bleak occasions.

One such deadly tsunami happened in the eastern Mediterranean at sunrise on July 21, 365 A.D. It began as a giant undersea earthquake. Geologists today believe the quake was a magnitude eight, or even higher. The shaker caused widespread damage, with nearly all of the towns in southern and central Greece destroyed, and much of Crete being leveled.

But the disaster would soon be followed by an even greater tragedy. First, the coastal waters retreated. Ships lay stranded on the wet sand. Then, the seas rose up in a mighty tsunami, which swamped the southern and eastern coasts of the Mediterranean. Libya, Alexandria, and the Nile Delta were especially hard hit. Thousands died in the earthquake and tsunami, and the high waves hurled ships about two miles inland. Carbon dating shows coral on the coast of Crete was lifted 30 feet out of the water in one massive push.

Some have suggested the quake and tsunami event

may be a collection of ancient disasters thrown into one story. Historians note writers of the time had a tendency to assess natural disasters as divine events. Authors such as church historian Sozomenus may have combined several tragedies to present the disaster as either divine sorrow, or wrath for the death of Emperor Julian, who had tried to stop the spread of Christianity and restore the Roman traditional religion two years earlier.

The tsunami was so devastating that the anniversary of the disaster was still being commemorated every year into the end of the sixth century in Alexandria.

Great Hurricane Tragedy

It's known simply as "The Great Hurricane Tragedy." A powerful and deadly storm that even impacted the American Revolution. It is the storm which holds the title of the most deadly Atlantic hurricane on record, with a shocking death toll of as many as 22,000 people.

The killer hurricane began as a tropical storm in October of 1780. It's exact origin is unknown, as hurricane records wouldn't be kept in the U.S. until 1850. It quickly began to strengthen and expand in size, moving westward toward the island of Barbados. Residents of the small island were first hit with a rainstorm on the night of October 9. Soon the full impact of the hurricane would be felt. There was no way at the time to measure the wind speed as the storm slammed Barbados. From the reported effects, the wind velocity may have been as great as Hurricane Camille in 1969, which, at 190 mph, has the highest measured, sustained wind speed at landfall of any hurricane.

Some of the first deaths included a clergyman and his family who hid from the storm in the church of St. Thomas. The heavy winds and rain proved to be disastrous, bringing the church down on top of the doomed family. At least four other churches were destroyed in the storm's fury; many others were severely damaged. Scores of homes and buildings on the island would not escape the hurricane's wrath, being blown down to rubble and killing many inside. The storm was so fierce that it even stripped bark off of trees, leaving none standing on the island. When it had finally passed, the death toll was an estimated 4,500.

The "Great Hurricane" then set it's sights on the island of Saint Vincent. Nearly all of the 600 houses in Kingstown were destroyed, and 19 Dutch ships were wrecked in the harbor at Grenada. It then moved to Saint Lucia, where the driving winds would lift a ship out of the water and on top of the city hospital, destroying the building. Another ship disappeared without a trace. In all, about 6,000 people perished.

Off the coast of Martinique sat a fleet of 40 French ships destined to do battle in the American Revolutionary war. The hurricane would decimate the fleet, causing the boats to capsize, and drowning an estimated 4,000 soldiers. The killer storm then developed a 25-foot storm surge which slammed the island of Saint-Pierre. There the death toll was the highest, an estimated 9,000 people dying at the hand of the unrelenting wind and rain.

The hurricane finally began to weaken, although it was still powerful enough to cause major damage in southern Puerto Rico, killing at least a thousand; and east Santo Domingo. It also grounded 50 ships near Bermuda. It made it's final stand in East Florida, hitting with furious winds and high tides, and causing coastal damage.

The hurricane was part of the disastrous 1780 Atlantic hurricane season, with two other deadly storms occurring in the same month. Those two accounted for at least two thousand total lives lost. It's the only time in U.S. history when three storms in one month terrorized the south, leaving high death tolls in each storm's wake.

Tri-State Tornado Tragedy

It was the deadliest tornado disaster in U.S. history. A storm so devastating it would take more than 700 lives in three states, and all in just a few short hours.

The ingredients for the deadly mix began to come together at about seven a.m. on March 17, 1925, over Montana. It would fuse with storms over Denver, Colorado, West Texas and northern New Mexico. By noon the next day, the deepening storm was gathered over south-central Missouri, and eastern Oklahoma. The first tornado was spotted in Shannon County, Missouri, at 12:40 p.m. It began as a small twister but quickly grew in size, causing it's first death at about one p.m. near the town of Ellington. It began to destroy homes and barns, setting it's sites on Annapolis. The tornado was destructive, leveling much of the town and killing two more people.

The tragic march had begun. The twister continued through the mining town of Leadanna, where it carried sheets of iron as far as 50 miles away; and into Bollinger County where it damaged two schools, injuring dozens of school kids. Multiple homes were also destroyed. As it crossed into Perry County, witnesses recalled seeing two large funnels in Biehle and Frohna. At least eleven people died altogether in Missouri.

The massive tornado then crossed the Mississippi River into southern Illinois, stripping the bark from trees and leaving a deep scar in the earth. At about 2:30 p.m. it smashed into the town of Gorham, ripping railroad tracks from the ground and obliterating homes and businesses, leaving 34 dead in it's wake. The mile-wide tornado then targeted Murphysboro, with tragic results. Along with sweeping away tracks of homes, the storm ripped through a railroad shop, killing 35; a school, killing 17 students; and another school, killing 9. Overall, 234 people died in Murphysboro, the most deaths in a single city in U.S. history by one tornado.

A school in DeSoto was the next target, with 33 students dying when a portion of the school collapsed. Further east, the mining town of West Frankfort suffered 152 fatalities, as entire subdivisions were swept away.

The tornado then literally wiped the town of Parrish off the map; 22 people died and the town was never rebuilt. In just 40 minutes, the tornado took 541 lives, and the death toll would rise to 613 people in Illinois before the storm finally left the state.

But the devastating was far from over. The tornado crossed the Wabash River into Indiana, demolishing the town of Griffin, killing 26. It destroyed half the town of Princeton, killing another 45 people. A Heinz factory was also badly damaged. The deadly storm finally dissipated shortly after 4:30 near the town of Petersburg. In all, 71 people, and possibly more, died in

Indiana. It left a deadly total of nearly 700 dead, and possibly more, with the majority in southern Illinois.

The tornado lasted a record three and a half hours.

Tri-State Tornado Tragedy

Part of the problem it presented was that it's appearance at times was not that of a normal funnel-shaped tornado, but rather a rolling fog that confused many farmers, who didn't take action until it was too late. At other times it was shrouded in heavy rain and even hail in some places. Some have suggested it may have been more than one tornado that caused all the damage; several other so- called "long track tornadoes" have been proven to be a family of tornadoes, and not just a single entity. But meteorologists note the conditions for the Tri-State Tornado appear to have been unique, which may have fueled the raging storm. Experts believe it was an F5 tornado, the strongest of all on the tornado scale. It also raced along at speeds of between 60 and 70 miles per hour, which made the powerful storm even more deadly.

Several memorials to the victims of the 1925 tornado can be found in all three states. One is a small boulder listing the names of the victims in Griffin, Indiana; names lost to time but not to history.

Sicily Tornadoes Tragedy

We often think of tornadoes as being confined to the middle section of the U.S. But this terrifying destructive force of nature is found all over the world. One such tornado disaster happened in Italy, and was comprised of two such deadly twisters.

It was fall of 1851. The people of western Sicily were experiencing stormy weather, when from out of the sky two dagger-like funnel clouds descended. The *Illustrated London News* later reported the tornadoes began as two waterspouts, which swept across the Sicilian plains from Marsala to Castellamare del Golfo. They evolved into a supercell of two full blown tornadoes, spinning only about 500 yards apart. The effect was devastating. Half the town of Castellamare was destroyed by the twin twisters, killing about 200.

The city harbor was heavily damaged, with many vessels destroyed or capsized. Dozens of crew members were lost at sea. It's believed the storm that produced the tornadoes was also a hurricane, and major damage was caused by the high winds and hail.

The total number of victims is unknown. But historians suggest more than 500 people were killed which is the highest death toll for a tornado in the history of continental Europe.

Earthquake Tragedies

Calcutta Cyclone Earthquake Tragedy

Earthquakes and cyclones have devastated the earth for centuries. But rarely do the two forces combine to create a disaster of epic proportions. Unfortunately for the city of Calcutta, India, the possible double dose of destruction proved to be a very real tragedy.

The date was October 11, 1737. Sailors in the region were going through their daily routine when they were stopped in their tracks by a surge of water coming right at them. Some said later they thought the wave was the result of a small earthquake. As many as two thousand homes in the English sector of town were reportedly thrown to the ground and destroyed by the surging water, and one church even sank into the ground without breaking apart. Some have suggested this may have been due to liquefaction caused by an earthquake.

The seaport was heavily damaged, with as many as 20,000 ships, boats, and canoes being washed away. The tidal surge was estimated at 30 feet. When it was through, the death toll was an astonishing 300,000 (although the population was believed to be at about 20,000, so the number of dead remains controversial; some of the excess may include unaccounted-for sailors). For those who lived in the region, almost all were left homeless; the homes were mostly made of mud with straw roofs, and dissolved in the surging water. The flood was powerful enough to knock down brick structures as well.

The disaster would come to be known as the Calcutta cyclone; later, when the name of the city changed to Kolkata, it would be called the Kolkata cyclone. But it was originally labeled the great Calcutta earthquake, and on some lists is still recognized as one of the more deadly earthquakes in modern history. Investigators have long wondered if the tragedy was the result of the double event of an earthquake and a deadly storm, or simply a mis- reported storm of great proportion. Over time, many researchers have come to the conclusion that the tidal surge was actually the result of a powerful cyclone, which reports of the day say hit at the mouth of the Ganges river on October 11. Of course, news was in its' infancy at that time, and many determined it was an earthquake simply by seeing the aftermath of the disaster. Other eyewitnesses claimed the flood waters had to have come from a storm that traveled up river. Researchers also note the Ganges River Delta is prone to tropical cyclones and flooding, with killer storms striking at least seven times in a 150 year period. But whether the tragedy was the result of a cyclone or a hurricane, or both, it remains one of the greatest natural causes of death in human history.

Antioch Quake Tragedy

Earthquakes are one of nature's most devastating forces. Combined with fire, the two can be extremely destructive. Sadly, those forces collided in 526 A.D., with tragic results.

The city of Antioch was part of the Byzantine Empire, in what is now the region of Syria. It was home to about half a million people. Antioch was the destination for St Paul's first missionary journey following his conversion on the Damascus road, and the New Testament tells us that its gentile converts to the new religion were also the first to call themselves Christians.

Sometime on a sunny morning in late May, the ground began to shake violently. An earthquake estimated at 7.0 slammed the city. Many of the buildings were immediately damaged in the severe quake, including Constantine's great octagonal church Domus Aurea. Only homes built at the base of the mountain survived the powerful earthquake.

As devastating as the quake was, fire began to overtake the city, spurred on by high winds. It would consume much of the area, causing most of the damage to Antioch. Even the great octagonal church would be lost to the flames. The fire burned for seven days; when it was finally out, little was left of the city. Even the harbor would be rendered unusable for ships, because the quake deposited tons of silt in the harbor.

In Constantinople, Justin the first sent money to help the citizens, and begin the reconstruction. The rebuilding of the great church was at the forefront of the efforts. But the scale of the damage was great. An estimated 250,000 people died in the quake and subsequent fire. It's been suggested the high mortality rate was due to a large number of people visiting at the time of the quake, to celebrate Ascension Day. The ground would continue shaking for another 18 months, as aftershocks riddled the area. The city would even be hit by another large killer quake in 528, although the death toll was far fewer.

Today, some of the ruins from the great earthquake can still be seen strewn about the ground. The quake would signal the end of the glory days of Antioch.

Shaanxi Earthquake Tragedy

It's known simply as the most deadly earthquake in recorded history. A quake so powerful the death toll is almost unimaginable, and of epic proportions, a disaster which boggles the mind.

The year was 1556 in China's province of Shaanxi.

On the evening of January 23, the ground began to shake violently. Witnesses said the quake was so violent that rivers would change direction; roads were destroyed; the ground in some areas rose up and formed new hills, or sank and became new sixty-foot deep valleys. New streams of water burst out of the ground. Experts believe the earthquake was an eight magnitude, making it especially deadly.

The death toll was staggering. The quake's epicenter was in the Wei River Valley, near the cities of Huaxian, Weinan and Huayin. In Huaxian, every building fell to the ground, reduced to rubble. More than half of the city's residents were killed, numbering in the hundreds of thousands. Other areas were also hammered by the powerful quake, which was felt more than 300 miles from the epicenter. Landslides triggered by the quake also contributed to the massive death toll. Millions of people at the time lived in caves on the high cliffs of Loess Plateau. The ground there was a soft clay which easily crumbled when the quake hit, and landslides destroyed the caves, killing hundreds of thousands. In all, an estimated 830,000 people died that day, or about 60 percent of the region's population. Experts blame the high death toll on the quake hitting in the middle of a densely populated area filled with poorly constructed buildings.

Later, some would suggest the earthquake may have been a form of punishment for people's sins, and some even suggested it could be a sign of the birth of the Antichrist. In any case, it was not only the worst earthquake in recorded time in terms of lives lost, it was also the worst disaster in history by a considerable margin, with the earthquake and tsunami in Indonesia ranking a distant second.

Epidemic Tragedies

Cocoliztli Plague Tragedy

It was the worst plague to ever hit what is now modern-day Mexico. An epidemic so disastrous it killed millions. And its' cause remains unknown.

It's known as the epidemics of 1545 and 1576, or the cocoliztli epidemic, for the collection of illnesses which caused the plague. It began after a long drought stretching from Venezuela to Canada. The rains which followed the drought appear to have increased the populations of the Vesper mouse, which carried a viral hemorrhagic fever.

Symptoms included high fever and severe headache, black tongue, and profuse bleeding from the nose, eyes, and mouth. Death would usually overtake the victim in three to four days.

The epidemic of 1545 covered all of Mexico, and claimed as many as 15,000,000 lives. It's believed about 80% of the Indian population was killed by the disease.

Another bout claimed 2,000,000 more in 1576. Of a total population estimated at about four and a half million, close to 45% died. Some cities were nearly wiped out; Tepeaca had a pre- epidemic population of 60,000, and a post-epidemic population of only 8,000. The area known as New Spain was left almost empty. Oddly enough, animals for the most part were not affected by the plague, with records showing only farm animals surviving in some towns. In each case, the plague lasted about two years before dispersing.

Experts today say the disease is difficult to link to any specific disease known today. It's believed an agent hosted in a rain-sensitive rodent environment was responsible, and that if not extinct, the microorganism that caused cocoliztli could reappear under favorable conditions.

Justinian Plague Tragedy

It was a plague rivaled only by the infamous "black death." A plague so devastating that it killed almost 15% of the world's population.

It's known as the "plague of Justinian," a pandemic which afflicted the Eastern Roman Empire, and was especially deadly in the capital of Constantinople. It began in 535 A.D. Investigators believe it was caused by extreme weather events and a global climate shift toward the later "Little Ice Age." DNA from human remains of the time reveal the first recorded instances of bubonic plague, and it's believed strains of the disease caused the deadly pandemic.

The outcome was catastrophic. While the total number of deaths is uncertain, it's believed as many as 25 million people perished from the Justinian plague. At it's peak, the disease killed 5000 people a day, and resulted in the deaths of about 40% of the city of Constantinople, and about one quarter of the population of the Eastern Mediterranean.

So how did it happen? Scholars speculate the disease was carried to Constantinople by infected rats on grain ships from Egypt. The earliest reports of the epidemic came in 541 from the port of Pelusium near Suez. Historians in Constantinople say there were so many casualties, there was no room to bury the dead. Bodies were left stacked out in the open, and funeral rites were often not held over the victims. It's long-term effects on European history were enormous. The plague weakened the Byzantine Empire at a critical point, when Justinian's armies had nearly retaken all of Italy and the western Mediterranean coast. The plague may have also contributed to the success of the Arabs a few generations later in the Byzantine-Arab wars.

The disease would continue to haunt the Eastern Mediterranean in the sixth, seventh, and eighth centuries, but became less and less virulent over time. But the total loss of life from the Justinian Plague tragedy would be one of the greatest in human history.

1918 Flu Pandemic Tragedy

It was the deadliest natural disaster ever to hit the earth. A flu so virulent it infected half a billion people around the world. As many as 100 million lives would be taken by the so-called "Spanish Flu."

The site of the first confirmed outbreak was at Fort Riley in Kansas. The first victim was diagnosed on March 11, 1918. Mess cook Private Albert Mitchell is considered the first patient, although some have suggested the flu originated in East Asia. In any case, the spread was instantaneous. In the U.S., the close quarters and massive troop movements of World War One helped spread the virus, and may have also allowed it to mutate into an even deadlier form. Many of the initial dead were soldiers, believed to have weakened immune systems due to malnourishment. World War One allies began to refer to the disease as the Spanish Flu, because it received greater attention in the press after moving from France to Spain in November of 1918.

The global mortality rate is not known, but experts suggest about 20% of those infected died. The disease may have killed 25 million in the first 25 weeks. Current estimates put the death toll somewhere between 50 million and 100 million. It may have killed even more people than the Black Death, and was found in every corner of the globe. In India alone, the death toll was over 13 million. In the U.S., as many as 675,000 died. Some victims bled from the ears. Oddly, most of the victims were young adults. This is unusual, because influenza is normally more deadly to weaker individuals, such as the elderly and infants.

1918 Flu Pandemic

One unusual side effect of the disease was a possible increase in aspirin poisoning deaths. One study discovered many people died after the U.S. Surgeon General recommended high doses of aspirin to fight the disease. Some researchers reject the theory, saying the death rates at the time in question were high even in places like India which had no access to aspirin. But others argue cheap quality aspirin was available to the Indian population.

The Spanish flu may have also tipped the balance of World War One. Some scholars note the virus hit the Central Powers before the Allied Powers, with mortality rates higher in Germany and Austria than in Britain and France.

Despite the huge loss of life, the Spanish flu began to fade from public awareness, and was labeled "the forgotten pandemic" until the news about bird flu in the 2000s.

Author's Note

I started this project after being inspired by another book I was writing, which also dealt with death. It occurred to me that in my lifetime there have been many tragedies to speak of, including the devastating losses of 9/11. But I began to wonder about the tragedies of the past that I had no knowledge of, that had impacted people as greatly as some of our recent tragedies have impacted us as a whole. I began to research the issue and found many tragedies that had eluded me in my lifetime, with details abounding on the internet. It seemed like it was time to chronicle these long-forgotten events, hence the title of this book.

I sincerely hope the readers will honor the memories of those lost in these stories, and remember that life is not to be taken for granted. Live and love with great fervor, because *tomorrow is not promised to anyone.*

Bibliography

1871 Peshtigo Fire
Hipke, Deana C.; "The Great Peshtigo Fire of 1871",
www.peshtigofire.info, Deana C. Hipke 2001
Wikipedia, "Peshtigo Fire"
https://en.wikipedia.org/wiki/Peshtigo_Fire Rosenfeld, Everett,
"The Peshtigo Fire 1871"
http://content.time.com/time/specials/packag
es/article/0,28804,2076476_2076484_20765   03,00.html   *Time*
Magazine, June 8, 2011

1904 General Slocum
Wingfield, Valerie; "The General Slocum Disaster of June 15,
1904; www.nypl.org/blog/2011/06/13/great-slocu m-disaster-
june-15-1904 NYC Neighborhoods, NY Public Library, June 13,
2011
Wikipedia, "PS General Slocum";
https://en.wikipedia.org/wiki/PS_General_Sl ocum, May 23, 2017

1918 Train Collision
Gendisasters.com, "Nashville, TN Train Wreck, Jul 1918, The Great
Train
Wreckof1918",http://www.gendisasters.com/tennessee/9204/nas
hville-tn-train-wreck-jul-1918 Gendisasters, Copyright 2003-2017
Wikipedia, "Great Train Wreck of 1918"
https://en.wikipedia.org/wiki/Great_Train_Wrec k_of_1918 July
2011

1928 Okeechopee
Brochu, Nicole Sterghos; "Florida's Forgotten Storm: The
Hurricane of 1928" http://www.sun-sentinel.com/sfl-ahurricane1
4sep14-story.html, Sun Sentinel, September 14, 2003
Wikipedia, "1928 Okeechobee Hurricane"
https://en.wikipedia.org/wiki/1928_Okeechobee_hurricane

Antioch Quake
Wikipedia, "526 Antioch Earthquake"
https://en.wikipedia.org/wiki/526_Antioch_earth quake February
12 2017
Wikipedia, "115 Antioch Earthquake"
https://en.wikipedia.org/wiki/115_Antioch_ earthquake
December 21 2016
Devastating Disasters, "Antioch Earthquake"
http://devastatingdisasters.com/antioch-earth quake/ March 20
2015

Balloon Bomb

Rizzo, Johnna, "Japan's Secret WWII Weapon:Balloon Bombs"
http://news.nationalgeographic.com/news/2013/0 5/130527-
map-video-balloon-bomb-wwii-japane se-air-current-jet-stream/
National Geographic, May 27 2013
Wikipedia, "Fire Balloon"
https://en.wikipedia.org/wiki/Fire_balloon#Singl e_lethal_attack
May 19 2017
Klein, Christopher, "Attack of Japan's Killer WWII Balloons, 70 Years
Ago" History Channel, May 5 2015

Beer Flood

Johnson, Ben, "The London Beer Flood of 1814",
http://www.historic-uk.com/HistoryUK/HistoryofBritain/The-
London-Beer-Flood-of-18 14/, Historic UK, 2017
Wikipedia, "London Beer Flood",
https://en.wikipedia.org/wiki/London_Beer_Floo d, May 25 2017
Klein, Christopher, "The London Beer Flood",
http://www.history.com/news/the-london-beer-flood-200-years-
ago, History, October 17, 2014

Calcutta Quake Cyclone

Traylor, Dean, "Earthquake or Cyclone: What Destroyed Calcutta
in 1737?", https://hubpages.com/education/Earthquake-
of-Cyclone-What-Destoryed-Calcutta-in-17 37, Hubpages, March
31, 2017
Bilham, Roger, "The 1737 Calcutta Earthquake and Cyclone
Evaluated", http://www.bssaonline.org/content/84/5/165 0.refs,
BSSA, October 1994
Hurricanes: Science and Society, "1737- Hooghly River",
http://www.hurricanescience.org/history/stor
ms/pre1900s/1737/, 2010-2015

Carolean Death March

MilitaryWikia, "Carolean Death March",
http://military.wikia.com/wiki/Carolean_De ath_March,
MilitaryWikia.com
Wikipedia, "Carolean Death March",
https://en.wikipedia.org/wiki/Carolean_Deat h_March, November
30 2016.

Child In Well

Wikipedia, "Kathy Fiscus",
https://en.wikipedia.org/wiki/Kathy_Fiscus, May 3 2017
Horton, Linda, "San Marino CA Child Falls Into Abandoned Well,
Apr 1949, http://www.gendisasters.com/california/195 11/san-
marino-ca-child-falls-abandoned-wel l-apr-1949, GenDisasters,
2003-2017Church Stampede
Wikipedia, "Shiloh Baptist Church Stampede",

https://en.wikipedia.org/wiki/Shiloh_Baptist

Church Stampede

Church_stampede, February 12 2017 Beitler, Stu, "Birmingham, AL
Baptist Church
Disaster, Sept 1902",
https://gendisasters.com/alabama/2451/birmi ngham%2C-al-
baptist-church-disaster%2C-s ept-1902, GenDisasters, 2003-2017
World Atlas, "The Shiloh Baptist Church Stampede of 1902",
http://www.worldatlas.com/articles/what-ha ppened-during-the-
shiloh-baptist-church-sta mpede.html, March 22 2017

Circus Fire

The Hartford Circus Fire-July 6, 1944,
http://www.circusfire1944.com/, circusfire1944@sbcglobal.net
Wikepedia, "Hartford Circus Fire",
https://en.wikipedia.org/wiki/Hartford_circu s_fire, May 27 2017
History, "The Hartford Circus Fire" http://www.history.com/this-
day-in-history/t he-hartford-circus-fire, A&E Television Networks,
2017

Circus Train Crash

Grey, Orrin, "Showmen's Rest: The DeadlyHammond Circus Train
Wreck of 1918", https://the-line-up.com/showmens-rest/, The
Line-up, January 12 2016
Wikipedia, "Hammond Circus Train Wreck",
https://en.wikipedia.org/wiki/Hammond_Cir cus_Train_Wreck,
October 30 2016

Cocoanut Grove Fire

Cocoanut Grove Coalition, "The Cocoanut Grove Fire",
http://www.cocoanutgrovefire.org/, November 2012
Wikipedia, "Cocoanut Grove Fire",
https://en.wikipedia.org/wiki/Cocoanut_Gro ve_fire, May 27 2017
NFPA Journal, "The Cocoanut Grove Fire",
http://www.nfpa.org/public-education/by-to pic/property-type-
and-vehicles/nightclubs-as sembly-occupancies/the-cocoanut-
grove-fire NFPA, 2016
,Cocoliztli Plague
Acuna-Soto, Rodolfo, Stahle, David, Cleaveland, Malcolm,
Therrell, Matthew; "Megadrought and Megadeath in 16 Century
Mexico", https://www.ncbi.nlm.nih.gov/pmc/articles/
PMC2730237/ PMC, April 8 2002
Wikipedia, "1576 Cocoliztli
Epidemic,https://en.wikipedia.org/wiki/1576_Cocoliztli_epide
mic, January 30 2017

Crete Tsunami

Fleury, Maureen, England, Prof. Philip, Friedman, Carla, "Crete

210

Earthquake of 365 AD",
https://worldhistoryproject.org/365/7/21/cret e-earthquake-of-365-ad, World History Project, 2017
Wikipedia, 365 Crete Earthquake,
https://en.wikipedia.org/wiki/365_Crete_earthquake
May 11 2017
Polonia, Alina, Bonatti, Enrico, Camerlenghi, Angelo, Lucchi,
Renata, Panieri, Giuliana, Gasperini, Luca, "Mediterranean
Megaturbidite Triggered by the AD 365 Crete Earthquake and
Tsunami", https://www.nature.com/articles/srep01285,
Squarespace, February 15, 2013

CSUF Massacre

Luppi, Kathleen, "40 Years Since a 5-minute Shooting Spree
Caused a Lifetime of Devastation, Cal State Fullerton Remembers 7
Lives Lost," http://www.latimes.com/socal/weekend/new s/tn-wknd-et-0703-cal-state-fullerton-memo rial-20160702-story.html, LA Times, July 12016
Wikipedia, "California State University, Fullerton Massacre",
https://en.wikipedia.org/wiki/California_Stat
e_University,_Fullerton_massacre, March 30 2017
Orange County Register, "40 Years On, Shooting Victims
Remembered at Cal State Fullerton Vigil", July 13 2016

Deadly Tiger

Dieselpokers, "The Legendary Champawat Tiger Was Responsible
For Killing 430 People" http://zazenlife.com/2012/07/22/the-legenda ry-champawat-tiger-was-responsible-for-kill ing-430-people/, July 22, 2012
Wikipedia, "Champawat Tiger,"
https://en.wikipedia.org/wiki/Champawat_T iger, May 5 201

Dyaltov Mystery

Morphy, Rob, "Mountain of the Dead: The Dyatlov Pass Incident",
http://mysteriousuniverse.org/2012/01/moun tain-of-the-dead-the-dyatlov-pass-incident/, Mysterious Universe, January 10 2012
Wikipedia, "Dyatlov Pass Incident",
https://en.wikipedia.org/wiki/Dyatlov_Pass_ incident, June 1 2017
Rennell, Tony, "Secret Soviet Death Rays. Yetis.
Aliens. Just What Did Slaughter Nine Hikers on Siberia's Death
Mountain in 1959?" UK Daily Mail, August 23 2013

Elephant Stampede

Unsolved Mystery, "The Chandka Forest Elephant Stampede-Top
10 Bizarre Disasters",
http://www.unsolved-mystery.com/2140, mynewswire.co, August 24 2011
Survivallife.com, "The 11 Weirdest Disasters in Human History",

https://survivallife.com/weirdest-disasters/, Above Average Joe, 2017

Wirth, Jennifer, "10 Bizarre Disasters History Forgot About" https://survivallife.com/weirdest-disasters/, Allday, 2017

First School Shooting

Wikipedia, "Enoch Brown School Massacre", https://en.wikipedia.org/wiki/Enoch_Brown school_massacre, March 22 2017 Strait, Megan, "Enoch Brown: A Massacre Unmatched", http://pabook2.libraries.psu.edu/palitmap/En och.html, Pabook, Fall 2010

Fort Dix Tragedies

Beitler, Stu, "Ft. Dix, NJ 45 Die in Military Plane Crash, July 1956" http://www.gendisasters.com/new-jersey/39 39/ft.-dix%2C-nj-45-die-military-plane-cras h%2C-july-1956, GenDisasters.com, 2003-2017

Maag, Christopher, "Garden State of Mind: Remembering a Forgotten Military Tragedy in New Jersey", http://www.northjersey.com/story/news/colu mnists/christopher-maag/2017/05/28/garden -state-mind-remembering-forgotten-military -tragedy-new-jersey/345782001/, NorthJersey.com, May 28, 2017 Beitler, Stu, "Fort Dix, NJ Navy Fighter Crashes Into Airliner, July 1949", http://www.gendisasters.com/new-jersey/46 02/fort-dix%2C-nj-navy-fighter-crashes-airl iner%2C-july-1949, GenDisasters.com, 2003-2017

Grand Canyon Plane Tragedy

Wikipedia, "1956 Grand Canyon Mid-Air Collision", https://en.wikipedia.org/wiki/1956_Grand_ Canyon_mid-air_collision, May 11 2017 Federal Aviation Administration, "TWA Lockheed Constellation and UAL DC-7Collision Over Grand Canyon, AZ, http://lessonslearned.faa.gov/ll_main.cfm?T abID=3&LLID=50&LLTypeID=2, FAA, 2017

Great Hurricane 1780

Wikipedia, "Great Hurricane of 1780", https://en.wikipedia.org/wiki/Great_Hurrica ne_of_1780, May 22 2017 *Encyclopaedia Britannica* Editors, "Great Hurricane of 1780", https://www.britannica.com/event/Great-hur ricane-of-1780, *Encyclopaedia Britannica*, 2017 History Channel, "Deadliest Atlantic Hurricane Hits", http://www.historychannel.com.au/this-day- in-history/deadliest-atlantic-hurricane-hits/, History, 2017

Hurricane Camille Tragedy
https://en.wikipedia.org/wiki/Hurricane_Camille
http://hurricanescience.org/history/storms/1960s/camille/
http://www.nhc.noaa.gov/outreach/history/#camille

Johnstown Flood
Wikipedia, "Johnstown Flood",
https://en.wikipedia.org/wiki/Johnstown_Flood, May 29 2017
McCullough, David, "An Overview of the 1889 Tragedy",
http://www.jaha.org/attractions/johnstown-flood-museum/flood-history/, JAHA, 2017

Justinian PlagueHorgan, John, "Justinian's Plague",
http://www.ancient.eu/article/782/, *Ancient History Encyclopedia*, December 26 2014
Wikipedia, "Plague of Justinian",
https://en.wikipedia.org/wiki/Plague_of_Just inian, May 10 2017
Tharoor, Ishaan, "The Plague of Justinian",
http://content.time.com/time/specials/packag
es/article/0,28804,2027479_2027486_20275 46,00.html, *Time*,
October 26 2010

L.A. Dam Failure
Harrison, Scott, "California Retrospective St.
Francis Dam Collapse Left a Trail of Death and Destruction",
http://www.latimes.com/local/california/la- me-stfrancis-dam-retrospective-20160319-st ory.html, *LA Times,* March 19 2016
Wikipedia, "St. Francis Dam",
https://en.wikipedia.org/wiki/St._Francis_D am, March 23 2017

Lancastria
Dancocks, Raye, "The Lancastria-a secret Sacrifice in World War Two" http://www.bbc.co.uk/history/worldwars/w
wtwo/lancastria_01.shtml, BBC, February 02 2017
Chapman, James, "Sinking of the Lancastria
Marked at Last", www.dailymail.co.uk/news/article-3128991/Sink
ing-Lancastria-marked-Wartime-loss-troop-ship- cost-4-000-lives-commemorated-75-years-on.ht ml, Daily Mail UK, June 17 2015
Wikipedia, *"RMS Lancastria",*
https://en.wikipedia.org/wiki/RMS_Lancastr ia, April 23 2017

London School Blast
New York Daily News, "New London School Explosion Kills Hundreds of Children in 1937",
http://www.nydailynews.com/news/national/ new-london-school-explosion-kills-hundred s-children-1937-article-1.3000047
Originally Published by the Daily News on March 19 1937
Wikipedia, "New London School

Explosion"https://en.wikipedia.org/wiki/Ne
w_London_School_explosion, May 13 2017

Mining Disaster

Editors of *Encyclopaedia Britannica*, "Monongah Mining Disaster
of 1907", https://www.britannica.com/event/Mononga h-mining-
disaster-of-1907, 2007
Wikipedia, "Monongah Mining Disaster,"
https://en.wikipedia.org/wiki/Monongah_mining_disaster, April 4
2017
WV A&H, "Monongah Mine Disaster",
http://www.wvculture.org/history/disasters/ monongah03.html
From the Illustrated Monthly West Virginian, January 1908

Molasses Flood

Trex, Ethan, "Boston's Great Molasses Flood of 1919"
http://mentalfloss.com/article/27366/bostons
-great-molasses-flood-1919, Mental Floss, 2011
Wikileaks, "Great Molasses Flood",
https://en.wikipedia.org/wiki/Great_Molasse s_Flood, April 22
2017
Celebrate Boston, "Boston Molasses Flood, 1919",
http://www.celebrateboston.com/disasters/m olasses-flood.htm
Copyright 2016

Mt. Pelee Eruption

McKie, Robin, "Three Minutes of Horror When 30,000 Perished"
https://www.theguardian.com/world/2002/a
pr/28/physicalsciences.highereducation, The Guardian, April 28
2002
Wikipedia, "Mount Pelee",
https://en.wikipedia.org/wiki/Mount_Pel%C
3%A9e, May 21 2017
Rosen, Julia "Benchmarks: May 8, 1902: The Deadly Eruption"
https://www.earthmagazine.org/article/benc hmarks-may-8-
1902-deadly-eruption-mount
-pelee, Earth Magazine, May 2015

On-air Suicide

Lost Media Archive, "Christine Chubbuck Suicide Video",
http://lostmediaarchive.wikia.com/wiki/Chri
stine_Chubbuck_Suicide_Video_(Recorded
_in_1974), 2017
Wikipedia, "Christine Chubbuck",
https://en.wikipedia.org/wiki/Christine_Chu bbuck, May 30 2017
News.com.au, "You're Going to see Another First, Attempted
Suicide", http://www.news.com.au/entertainment/mov
ies/upcoming-movies/youre-going-to-see-an other-first-

attempted-suicide-the-onair-suici de-of-news-reporter-christine-
chubbuck/ne ws-story/769d8bcc4d90cf072bf7b3ed23e38 b49,
January 27 2016

Picnic Train Crash

Thomas, JD, "The Picnic Train Tragedy of 1856",
http://www.accessible-archives.com/2013/0
7/the-picnic-train-tragedy-of-1856/, Accessible Archives, July 17
2013

Wikipedia, "The Great Train Wreck of 1856",
https://en.wikipedia.org/wiki/Great Train Wreck_of_1856, May
28 2017

School Bomb

Evon, Dan, "1927 School Bombing Was The Deadliest in American
History", http://www.inquisitr.com/442729/1927-scho ol-
bombing-was-deadliest-in-american-histo ry/, Inquisitr, December
17 2012

Wikipedia, "Bath School Disaster",
https://en.wikipedia.org/wiki/Bath_School_ disaster, June 1 2017

Peters, Justin, "We Still Look at Ourselves as Survivors",
http://www.slate.com/blogs/crime/2012/12/1
8/bath_school_bombing_remembering_the_
deadliest_school_massacre_in_american.ht ml, Slate, December 18
2012

School Bus Accident

Jebavy, Sharon Young, "Big Sandy Bus Accident 1958",
http://www.rootsweb.ancestry.com/~kyjohn so/Bus.htm,
Ancestry.com, 2017

Wikipedia, "Prestonburg, Kentucky Bus Disaster",
https://en.wikipedia.org/wiki/Prestonsburg,_
Kentucky_bus_disaster, March 13 2017

Copley, Rich, "Film Depicts an Appalachian Tragedy"
http://www.kentucky.com/entertainment/mo vies-news-
reviews/article44023902.html, Lexgo, February 21 2010

Shaanxi Earthquake

Harris, Colin, "Shaanxi Earthquake",
https://worldhistoryproject.org/1556/1/23/sh aanxi-earthquake,
World History Project, May 12 2008

Wikipedia, "1556 Shaanxi Earthquake",
https://en.wikipedia.org/wiki/1556_Shaanxi
_earthquake, May 29 2017

Editors, *Encyclopedia Britannica*, "Shaanxi Province Earthquake of
1566",

Sicily Tornadoes

Robinson, Claudia, "The 1851 Sicily Tornades"

https://prezi.com/7a40gp30cje1/the-1851-sic ily-tornades/, **Prezi,**
April 22 2016
Wikipedia, "Sicily Tornadoes",
https://en.wikipedia.org/wiki/Sicily_Tornad oes, **May 22 2017**

Spanish Flu

Billings, Molly, "The Influenza Pandemic of 1918",
https://virus.stanford.edu/uda/#top,
Stanford Education, June 1997 Modified February 2005
Wikipedia, "1918 Flu Pandemic"
https://en.wikipedia.org/wiki/1918_flu_pand emic, **May 31 2017**
Latson, Jennifer, "What Made the Spanish Flu so Deadly?"
http://time.com/3731745/spanish-flu-history
/, **Time, March 11 2015**

St. Felix Flood

Deltawerken.com, "Saint Felix Flood",
http://www.deltawerken.com/St.-Felixflood- (1530)/497.html,
2014
Wikipedia, "St. Felix Flood",
https://en.wikipedia.org/wiki/St._Felix%27s
_flood, **November 13 2016**
Dr. Zar, "The Flood That Destroyed a City",
http://www.historyandheadlines.com/flood- destroyed-dutch-
city/, History & Headlines, November 5

Sultana Steamboat

Ambrose, Stephen, "Remembering Sultana",
http://news.nationalgeographic.com/news/20
01/05/0501_river5.html, National Geographic News, May 1 2001
Wikipedia, "Sultana Steamboat",
https://en.wikipedia.org/wiki/Sultana_(stea
mboat), **May 30 2017**
Hamilton, Jon, "The Shipwreck That Led Confederate Veterans To
Risk All For Union Lives,
http://www.npr.org/2015/04/27/402515205/t he-shipwreck-that-
led-confederate-veterans- to-risk-all-for-union-lives, NPR, April
27 2015

Theater Fire

Crimmins, Jerry, "Iroquois Theater Fire of 1903 Is Still the Worst of
Chicago's Deadly Blazes,"
http://articles.chicagotribune.com/1993-03-1
7/news/9303170288_1_worst-fires-early-mo rning-fire-terrible-
fires, *Chicago Tribune*, March 17 1993
Wikipedia, "Iroquois Theater Fire",
https://en.wikipedia.org/wiki/Iroquois_Theat re_fire, **April 3 2017**
History Bits, "Iroquois Theater Fire",

http://www.historybits.com/iroquois-theatre- fire.htm, ThorFire Enterprises, 2017

Train Avalanche

History Channel, "Trains Buried by Avalanche", http://www.history.com/this-day-in-history/t rains-buried-by-avalanche, History 2017

Wikipedia, "Wellington, Washington",http

Bos, Carole, "The Wellington Disaster- America's Worst Avalanche",

s://e n.wi kipe dia. org/ wiki/We llin gton

,_W ashi ngto n#1 910_av alan che, Mar ch 20

2017https://www.awesomestories.com/asset/view /The-Wellington-Disaster-America-s-Worst- Avalanche, Awesome Stories, December 19

2013

Train Bridge Tragedy

Waymarking.com, "1904 Train Wreck-Eden, Colorado-Railway Disaster Sites on Waymarking.com",

http://www.waymarking.com/waymarks/W M60W4_1904_Train_Wreck_Eden_Colora do, Groundspeak, 2017

Wikipedia, "Eden Train Wreck",

https://en.wikipedia.org/wiki/Eden_train_wr eck, October 16 2016

Gendisasters, "Eden, CO Train Disaster, Aug 1904,

http://www.gendisasters.com/colorado/5747 /eden-co-train-disaster-aug-1904, 2017

Tri-state Tornado

History Channel, "The Tri-State Tornado", http://www.history.com/this-day-in-history/t he-tri-state-tornado, A&E Television Networks, 2017

Wikipedia, "Tri-State Tornado", https://en.wikipedia.org/wiki/Tri-State_Torn ado, 2017

Hyde, James, "The Tri-State Tornado of 1925" http://www.ustornadoes.com/2014/03/18/the -tri-state-tornado-of-1925/, U.S. Tornadoes, March 18 2014

Tyrolean Avalanches

Larson, S., Tyrolean Alps Avalanche of 1916, https://prezi.com/8oeiarevv3cl/tyrolean-alps-avalanche-of-1916/, Prezi, January 23 2014 Rosenberg, Jennifer, "10,000 Soldiers Die In Tyrol From Avalanches During World War I", https://www.thoughtco.com/soldiers-die-in-t yrol-avalanches-1779211, Thoughtco, January 7 2016

Wikipedia, History of Tyrol,

https://en.wikipedia.org/wiki/History_of_Ty rol, May 19 2017

Walkway Collapse

The Engineer, "Hyatt Regency Walkway Collapse",
http://www.engineering.com/Library/Article
sPage/tabid/85/ArticleID/175/Hyatt-Regenc y-Walkway-
Collapse.aspx, Engineering.com, October 24 2006
Wikipedia,"Hyatt Regency Walkway Collapse",
https://en.wikipedia.org/wiki/Hyatt_Regenc
y_walkway_collapse, May 8 2017
Roe, Jason, "Hotel Horror", http://www.kchistory.org/week-
kansas-city- history/hotel-horror, Kansas City Public Library,
KC History, 2017

Wilheim Gustloff

Kappes, Irwin, "Wilhelm Gustloff-The Greatest Marine
Disaster in History... And Why You Probably Never Heard of
It", http://www.militaryhistoryonline.com/wwii/
articles/wilhelmgustloff.aspx, MilitaryHistoryOnline, July 6
2003
Wikipedia, "MV Wilhelm Gustloff",
https://en.wikipedia.org/wiki/MV_Wilhelm Begley, Sarah,
"The Forgotten Maritime Tragedy That Was 6 Times Deadlier
Than the Titanic", http://time.com/4198914/wilhelm-
gustloff-s alt-to-the-sea/, Time, January 29 2016

Yellow River Floods

Wikipedia, "1887 Yellow River Flood",
https://en.wikipedia.org/wiki/1887_Yellow_ River_flood,
May 28 2017
Editors of the *Encyclopaedia Britannica*, "Huang He Floods",
https://www.britannica.com/event/Huang-H e-floods,
Britannica, 2017
Geol 105, "Huang He (Yellow) River,
http://geol105naturalhazards.voices.wooster.edu/huang-he-
yellow-river/, Geol 105
Natural Hazards, November 5 2012

Yungay Avalanche

Prifti, D, "Yungay, Peru, 31 May 1970 Avalanche",
https://prezi.com/mnyvosqi-0bf/yungay-per u-31-may-1970-
avalanche/, Prezi, January 27 2014
Wikipedia, "1970 Ancash Earthquake",
https://en.wikipedia.org/wiki/1970_Ancash_ earthquake,
March 31 2017
Theriault, Annie, "Yungay 1970-2009: Remembering the
Tragedy of the Earthquake" Peruvian Times, May 31 2009